The Blaze Engulfs

JANUARY 1939 – DECEMBER 1941

By
Victoria Sherrow

Academic Editor:
Dr. William L. Shulman
President, Association of Holocaust Organizations
Director, Holocaust Resource Center & Archives, New York

Series Advisor:
Dr. Michael Berenbaum
President & CEO of Survivors of the
Shoah Visual History Foundation, Los Angeles

Series Editor:
Lisa Clyde Nielsen

Advisory Board:
Dr. Minton Goldman, Associate Professor of Political Science,
Northeastern University, Boston

Kathryn Schindler, Teacher, Laguna Niguel Middle School, California;
multicultural and tolerance educator

Kathryn Greenberg, Educational and public-administration specialist,
Chicago Department of Public Health, Division of School Health

Rachel Kubersky, BA Library Education, MPH

Joachim Kalter, Holocaust survivor

A   B L A C K B I R C H   P R E S S   B O O K
W O O D B R I D G E ,   C O N N E C T I C U T

Acknowledgments

Many people have given generously of their time and knowledge during the development of this series. We would like to thank the following people in particular: Genya Markon, and the staff at the United States Holocaust Memorial Museum Photo Archives—Leslie Swift, Sharon Muller, Alex Rossino, and Teresa Pollin—for their talented guidance; and Dr. Michael Berenbaum, currently President and CEO of the Survivors of the Shoah Visual History Foundation and formerly Director of the Research Institute at the U.S. Holocaust Memorial Museum for his valuable editorial input and support of our efforts.

Dr. William L. Shulman, President of the Association of Holocaust Organizations and the Holocaust Resource Center & Archives at Queensborough Community College, merits special mention. As the series academic editor—as well as the compiler of Books 7 and 8—Dr. Shulman's guidance, insight, and dedication went far beyond the call of duty. His deep and thorough knowledge of the subject gave us all the critical perspective we needed to make this series a reality.

Published by Blackbirch Press, Inc.
260 Amity Road
Woodbridge, CT 06525

web site: http://www.blackbirch.com
e-mail: staff@blackbirch.com

©1998 Blackbirch Press, Inc.
First Edition

Printed in the United States of America

10 9 8 7 6 5 4 3 2 1

Cover: Hitler visits Paris soon after his successful invasion of France in June 1940 (AP/Wide World Photos).

Library of Congress Cataloging-in-Publication Data

Sherrow, Victoria.
    The blaze engulfs : January 1939 to December 1941 / by Victoria Sherrow.
        p.   cm. — (Holocaust)
    Includes bibliographical references and index.
    Summary: Using primary source material along with historical narrative, explores the unique aspects and events in the period of the Holocaust between January 1939 and December 1941.
    ISBN 1-56711-202-1 (lib. bdg. : alk. paper)
    1. Holocaust, Jewish (1939–1945)—Juvenile literature. 2. Jews—Germany—History—1933–1945—Juvenile literature. [1. Holocaust, Jewish (1939–1945). 2. Jews—Germany—History—1933–1945. 3. World War, 1939–1945—Atrocities.] I. Title. II. Series: Holocaust (Woodbridge, Conn.)
D804.34.G74   1998
940.53'18—dc21
                                                   96-37216
                                                     CIP
                                                   AC

CONTENTS

Preface   4

Foreword by Dr. Michael Berenbaum   5

INTRODUCTION
"Fire and Sword"   9

JANUARY–AUGUST 1939
1 "A Long Night of Savagery"   17

AUGUST–DECEMBER 1939
2 "Close Your Eyes to Pity!"   29

DECEMBER 1939–APRIL 1940
3 "The Soil Bleeds"   41

APRIL–DECEMBER 1940
4 "We Shall Never Surrender"   51

JANUARY–DECEMBER 1941
5 "A Huge Game of Death"   61

Chronology of the Holocaust: 1933-1945   73
Glossary   74
Source Notes   75
Bibliography   77
Further Reading   78
Index   79

Preface

At the United States Holocaust Memorial Museum in Washington, D.C., a poignant documentary explores antisemitism and its role in the Holocaust. The film ends with these words:

THIS IS WHERE PREJUDICE CAN LEAD.

That somber warning has guided our work on this series.

The task of creating a series of books on the Holocaust seemed, at first, straightforward enough: We would develop an in-depth account of one of the most complex and compelling periods in human history.

But it quickly became clear to us that, on an emotional level, this series would not be straightforward at all. Indeed, the more work we did, the more we realized just how this subject wraps itself around everyone it touches. As we discussed content with our authors and advisors and began to select photographs and other documents for reproduction, several unanticipated and complicated issues arose.

The first major issue was pivotal, in that our decision would guide the content of the books: How should we choose to define the very term *Holocaust*? Many scholars of the Holocaust believe that the term should be used exclusively in reference to the approximately 6 million European Jews who were murdered by Nazis and their collaborators between 1933 and 1945. This is because no other group was singled out so systematically and relentlessly for genocide. Should the perhaps 4 million non-Jewish victims of the period—the Soviet prisoners of war, Romani (Gypsies), Jehovah's Witnesses, German and Austrian male homosexuals, and other groups—be discussed on the same level as the Jews? Ultimately—in philosophical agreement with the U.S. Holocaust Memorial Museum—we decided to focus our discussion primarily on the Jews but also to report the experiences of other victims.

Our second major decision had to do with how to present the material. How explicit should the books be in their written descriptions and photographic records of what was done to the victims? Perhaps never before have the brutalities of war and the consequences of prejudice and hatred been so extensively chronicled; perhaps never so eloquently and, at the same time, in such painful detail.

On this issue, we decided we would chronicle what happened, but try not to shock or horrify. Learning about the Holocaust should be disturbing—but there is a delicate line between informative realism and sensationalism. The most brutal accounts and documentation of the Holocaust can be found in many other sources; we believe that in our series, much of this story will be revealed through the powerful and moving images we have selected.

Yet another difficult issue was raised by our educational advisors: Was the Holocaust truly a singular historical event, uniquely qualified for such detailed study as is provided in this series? That it was an extraordinary period in history, there can be no denial—despite some misguided people's efforts to the contrary. Certainly, never before had an entire nation organized its power and mobilized itself so efficiently for the sole purpose of destroying human life. Yet the Holocaust was not unique in terms of the number of people murdered; nor was it unique in the brutality of the hatred on which it fed.

A subject such as this raises many questions. How could the Holocaust have happened? Could it have been prevented? How can we keep this from happening again? We have done our best to explore the questions we feel are most central. Ultimately, however, the most compelling questions to emerge from learning about the Holocaust are for each individual reader to answer.

Foreword

There is a paradox in the study of the Holocaust: The more distant we are from the Event, the more interest seems to grow. In the immediate aftermath of the Holocaust, horrific images were played in movie theaters on newsreels, which was how people saw the news in an era before television. Broadcasting on CBS radio, famed newscaster Edward R. Murrow said:

Permit me to tell you what you would have seen and heard had you been with me on Thursday. It will not be pleasant listening. If you are at lunch or have no appetite to hear of what Germans have done, now is a good time to turn off your radio, for I propose to tell you of Buchenwald.

Murrow described the sights and sounds of what he had experienced in the immediate aftermath of liberation, and his audience was appropriately horrified. Action was required, trials were soon held—an accounting for a deed that was beyond human comprehension, a crime beyond a name, that we now call the "Holocaust."

Shortly thereafter, interest waned. Other topics of the era took center stage—the Cold War, the Berlin blockade, the Korean War—and it seemed for a time that the Holocaust would be forgotten. In retrospect, we can surmise that the silence was a necessary response to such catastrophe. Distance was needed before we could look back and muster enough courage to confront an event so terrible.

No one could have imagined that, half a century after the Holocaust, museums such as the United States Holocaust Memorial Museum would be built and would attract millions of visitors each year. No one, too, would have guessed that

films such as *Schindler's List* would be seen by tens of millions of people throughout the world. No one could have foreseen that thousands of books would be published on the subject and courses in schools all over the world would be taught—that interest in this horrible chapter of history would intensify rather than recede with the passage of time.

Why study the Holocaust?

The answer is simple: Because it happened!

An event of such magnitude, a state-sponsored annihilation of an entire people—men, women, and children— must be confronted. Some people have portrayed the Holocaust as an aberration, a world apart from the ordinary world in which we dwell. Even the most eloquent of survivors, Elie Wiesel, calls it the "Kingdom of Night." Yet, to me the Holocaust is not an aberration, but an expression in the extreme of a common thread that runs through our civilization. And thus, not to confront the Event is not to probe the deep darkness that is possible within our world.

Because it happened, we must seek to understand the anguish of the victims— the men, women, and children who faced death and had impossible choices to make, and who could do so little to determine their fate. And we must seek to understand the neutrality and indifference of the bystanders around the world; and what caused the Allies—who were fighting a full-scale world war against the Germans and other Axis powers—to fail to address the "second war," the war against the Jews.

We must also seek to understand the all-too-few non-Jewish heroes of the Holocaust—the men, women, and children who opened their homes and their hearts and provided a haven for the victims; a place to sleep, a crust of bread, a kind word, a hiding place. What makes such goodness possible? Why were they immune to the infection of evil?

We must understand that the Holocaust did not begin with mass killing. Age-old prejudice led to discrimination, discrimination led to persecution, persecution to incarceration, incarceration to annihilation. And mass murder, which culminated with the killing of approximately 6 million Jews, did not begin with the Jews—nor did it encompass only the Jews. The state-sponsored murder of the physically and mentally disabled was a precursor to the Holocaust. It was in that killing process that gas chambers and crematoria were developed and refined, and the staff of the death camps were trained. Romani (commonly but incorrectly referred to as Gypsies) were killed alongside the Jews. Jehovah's Witnesses, German and Austrian male homosexuals, political prisoners and dissidents were also incarcerated in concentration camps, where many were murdered. Gentile and Jewish Poles were subjected to decimation and destruction of their national identity. Though many Jews suffered alone, abandoned and forgotten by the world, they were not the only ones to die.

The study of the Holocaust is not easy. We are often unclear about whose history is being taught: German history, Jewish history, American history, European history. And to understand it, we need to understand more than history. Other disciplines are essential, such as psychology and sociology, political science, philosophy and theology, and, most especially, ethics. When we study the Holocaust, we are forced to face evil, to confront experiences that are horrific and destructive. And even despite the tools of all these disciplines, we still may not understand. Comprehension may elude us.

With the renewed interest in the Holocaust—especially in North America—we have seen that the study of all these deaths is actually in the service of life; the study of evil actually strengthens decency and goodness. For us as free citizens, confronting this European event brings us a new recognition of the principles of constitutional democracy: a belief in equality and equal justice under law; a commitment to pluralism and toleration; a determination to restrain government by checks and balances and by the constitutional protection of "inalienable rights"; and a struggle for human rights as a core value.

The Holocaust shatters the myth of innocence and, at the same time, has implications for the exercise of power. Those who wrestle with its darkness know it can happen again—even in the most advanced, most cultured, most "civilized" of societies. But, if we are faithful to the best of human values, the most sterling of our traditions, then we can have confidence that it "won't happen here." These truths are not self-evident; they are precarious and, therefore, even more precious.

The Holocaust has implications for us as individuals. As we read these books, we can't help but ask ourselves, "What would I have done?" "If I were a Jew, would I have had the courage to resist—spiritually or militarily—and when?" "Would I have had the wisdom and the ability to flee to a place that offered a haven?" "Do I have a friend who would offer me a place of shelter, a piece of bread, a moment of refuge?" "What could I have done to protect my family, to preserve my life?"

We can't offer easy answers because the options were few, the pressures extreme, the conditions unbearable, and the stakes ultimate—life or death.

We may also ask ourselves even more difficult questions: "What prejudices do I have?" "Do I treat all people with full human dignity?" "Am I willing to discriminate against some, to scapegoat others?" "Am I certain—truly certain—that I could not be a killer? That I would not submit to the pressures of conformity and participate in horrible deeds or, worse yet, embrace a belief that makes me certain—absolutely certain—that I am right and the others are wrong? That my cause is just and the other is an enemy who threatens me, who must be eliminated?" These are questions you will ask as you read these books—ask, but not answer.

Perhaps, in truth, the more intensely you read these books, the less certainty you will have in offering your personal answer. Premature answers are often immature answers. Good questions invite one to struggle with basic values.

The central theme of the story of the Holocaust is not regeneration and rebirth, goodness or resistance, liberation or justice, but, rather, death and destruction, dehumanization and devastation, and above all, loss.

The killers were "civilized" men and women of an advanced culture. They were both ordinary and extraordinary, a true cross-section of the men and women of Germany, its allies, and their collaborators, as well as the best and the brightest. In these volumes, those deeds will be seen, as will the evolution of policy, the expansion of the power of the state, and technological and scientific murders unchecked by moral, social, religious, or political constraints. Whether restricted to the past or a harbinger of the future, the killers demonstrated that systematic mass destruction is possible. Under contemporary conditions, the execution of such a policy would only be easier.

The Holocaust transforms our understanding. It shatters faith—religious faith in God and secular faith in human goodness. Its truth has been told not to provide answers, but to raise questions. To live conscientiously in its aftermath, one must confront the reality of radical evil and its past triumphs. At the same time, we must fight against that evil and its potential triumphs in the future.

The call from the victims—from the world of the dead—is to remember. From the survivors, initial silence has given way to testimony. The burden of memory has been transmitted and thus shared. From scholars, philosophers, poets, and artists—those who were there and those who were not—we hear the urgency of memory, its agony and anguish, its meaning and the absence of meaning. To live in our age, one must face the void.

Israel Ba'al Shem Tov, the founder of Hasidism, once said:

*In forgetfulness is the root of exile.
In remembrance, the seed of redemption.*

His fears of forgetting, we understand all too well.

Whether we can share his hope of remembrance is uncertain.

Still, it is up to us to create that hope.

Michael Berenbaum
Survivors of the Shoah
Visual History Foundation
Los Angeles, California

"Fire and Sword"

On the night of November 9, 1938, Manny Gale and his father were returning home to Trebitz, in eastern Germany, after being out of town for a short visit with relatives. As they approached their hometown, 14-year-old Manny saw flames. Worried that their house was burning, his father drove quickly. But at the entrance to Trebitz, a group of men wearing brown uniforms, their armbands displaying swastikas—the symbol of Adolf Hitler's Nazi regime— stopped them. These men, who included the mayor and chief of police, ordered Manny and his father out of their car, then took the car away. Confused and frightened, the Gales set out on foot. The mayor shouted after them, "We wish you luck, if you live through the night." It was a night of government-planned violence that would become known as *Kristallnacht*.

Hitler salutes hundreds of thousands of Nazi youths from his car in Nuremberg, 1935.

Once in the town, the Gales were shocked: Their house of worship—the synagogue—was a mass of flames. Hundreds of windows were broken, and glass littered the streets. Someone had stuck a sign above the shoemaker's door that said, LET THE JEW CROAK. A truck moved down the street, the Nazis inside yelling, "Destroy everything Jewish. Let nothing remain." Armed thugs grabbed Mr. Gale and forced him to crawl on his knees to the synagogue to join other men, all of them chained together. While the building burned, the town band played a merry waltz.

The frenzied violence then swept into people's homes. A mob carrying rifles broke through the Gales' door and used pipes and crowbars to destroy furniture, paintings, dishes—everything in sight. Outside, Manny's grandfather was savagely beaten. Manny's father was taken by force to a German concentration (labor) camp called Buchenwald.

The Gales were hard-working, law-abiding people. Mr. Gale was both a patriotic German and a World War I hero. But all of these things seemed to have been forgotten overnight. The Gales were Jews. And in Nazi Germany, being Jewish meant that a person had no civil rights, no protection under the law.

When Mr. Gale came home six weeks later, he walked with a limp and had a broken elbow and nose. The Nazis had decided to release veterans of World War I who had received medals. There was one condition: Manny's father was ordered to leave the country within six weeks or he would be imprisoned again.

A Swift Rise

Adolf Hitler had risen to power in Germany quickly, during turbulent times. In the 1920s, when he began his ascendancy, the country was mired in an economic depression. Millions of citizens were hungry and out of work. The national spirit of a once-proud people was low. The Germans were enraged by their loss of World War I and were humiliated by the terms they were forced to accept in the 1919 Treaty of Versailles. As part of the peace treaty, the Allies—led by the United States, France, Great Britain—

held Germany responsible for the war's vast destruction and millions of deaths. Germany was also forced to give up territory, slash its military, and pay billions of dollars in reparations for the damage it caused during the war.

Hitler used his nation's despair and humiliation as fuel for a new political movement, which took shape as the Nazi Party. Criticizing what he saw as a weak and ineffective government, the aspiring leader found that he could arouse strong reactions with his speeches. With great emotion and conviction, he pledged to all that he could return Germany to its prior greatness.

Early in 1933, he achieved his goal of gaining political power. On January 30, President Paul von Hindenburg swore Hitler in as Germany's new chancellor. One month later, Hitler assumed emergency powers, on the pretext that Communists—enemies of the Nazis—had set fire to the Reichstag (the German Parliament). Hitler then took charge of the armed forces, the police, and other institutions.

In 1934, upon the death of von Hindenburg, Hitler became president as well as chancellor. Eventually, he would be called the *Führer*, or "leader."

Overnight Transformation

Almost immediately upon taking power, Hitler's government enlarged the *Sturmabteilungen*, or SA—a military group known as stormtroopers or brown-shirts—to 400,000. The stormtroopers attacked people who opposed the Nazis, often right on the streets. They targeted Jews in particular, whom Hitler called "enemies" of the German people. (At the time, there were about 500,000 Jews in Germany, less than 1 percent of the population.)

Antisemitism—hatred of Jews—was a major part of Nazism. Hitler expressed contempt for Jews in his speeches and writings. He used them as scapegoats, blaming them for Germany's defeat in World War I, even though some 100,000 Jews had fought for Germany. Of those people, approximately 12,000 had died in the war, and 40,000 had won medals for bravery.

Antisemitism was a centuries-old phenomenon. Jews in Europe had always been a minority. They sometimes had to struggle for legal protection and the right to practice their religion freely. In some countries, Jews could not own land, attend school, or practice certain professions. By the 1930s, Jews had lived in Germany for many centuries and had contributed greatly to its culture. But these contributions meant little to most of the citizens of the Third Reich, the name that Hitler applied to his "empire."

In March 1933, Josef Goebbels, whom Hitler had appointed leader of the Nazi propaganda effort, announced a boycott of all Jewish businesses, to be held on April 1. Nazi supporters in the crowd yelled, "Hang them [the Jews]! Hang them!" Stormtroopers harassed Jews on the street, vandalized their shops and businesses, and posted signs that read JEWS PERISH and NO JEWS OR DOGS ALLOWED. A Jewish mother trying to buy bread for her family would find a sign on a shop's door that said NO JEWS.

Non-Citizens

In 1935, the government passed a series of anti-Jewish laws, which would become known as the Nuremberg Laws. These laws stripped Jews of their civil rights. They were forbidden to marry or have relations with non-Jews; nor could they vote, hold public office, or use public parks and other facilities. Jews were removed from government jobs.

By 1938, further restrictions were in place. Jews could not own radios or pets, earn a living, or attend school. Laws restricted where and how they could live and travel. Those who wanted to leave the country were allowed to take only a few personal belongings and about $10 in cash. Jewish property was seized.

From the start, the Nazis crushed nearly all resistance. Concentration camps—Dachau and Osthofen for men and Moringen for women—were set up in Germany as early as 1933, within weeks of Hitler coming to power. Within a year, there were 50 such prisons for Communists and other political opponents of the Nazis, dissenting Catholic and Protestant clergy, Jehovah's

Witnesses, Romani (commonly but incorrectly called Gypsies), Jews, and others. New camps were being built on a regular basis. People were imprisoned for writing or for distributing anti-Nazi literature. Criticizing the Nazis was also a crime. Children were urged to spy on their parents; neighbors were encouraged to report their neighbors if they overheard criticism of Hitler's regime.

Hitler and other high-ranking Nazis review a military parade held to honor the annexation of Austria by Germany, 1938.

"Utter Madness"

Hatred burst forth with highly organized and widescale acts of violence in 1938. In March, German troops marched into Austria to annex it for the Reich. This event, called the *Anschluss*, was welcomed by most Austrians.

But some eyewitnesses in Austria described horrifying acts, calling the scenes "utter madness." Jews were degraded, attacked, and arrested in the streets. Nazis beat old men and pulled out their beards. They forced Jews to crawl on the ground and eat grass or scrub public toilets.

Thousands of Jews fled Austria in terror. Some, in desperation, killed themselves.

Even worse violence followed. Nazi officials had long been planning a massive pogrom—a group or mob attack—against Jews and their property. The Nazis found an excuse to launch this pogrom when, in October 1938, a teenager named Herschel Grynszpan shot a Nazi official in Paris, in revenge for the deportation of his parents and thousands of other Polish Jews to camps. On the night of November 9, Nazi stormtrooper groups throughout Germany and Austria were ordered to destroy as many Jewish

KEY

The Third Reich, 1938

Annexed by Germany, 1938

North Sea

Baltic Sea

SWEDEN

Riga
LATVIA

LITHUANIA
Vilnius•

EAST PRUSSIA

HOLLAND
Amsterdam•

BELGIUM
Brussels•

Berlin•

GERMANY

SUDETENLAND

•Prague

CZECHOSLOVAKIA

•Warsaw

POLAND

•Cracow

•Paris

LUX.

FRANCE

Munich•

Vienna•

AUSTRIA

•Budapest

HUNGARY

•Bern
SWITZERLAND

ITALY

Europe by January 1, 1939

YUGOSLAVIA

ROMANIA

•Belgrade

homes, stores, businesses, and synagogues as possible and to attack Jews however they wished. Jewish men were to be arrested and sent to concentration camps. Police were not to interfere.

When November 10 dawned, thousands of Jewish shops were in ashes and rubble. Shattered glass lay on thousands of streets across Germany. More than 1,000 synagogues had been desecrated, damaged, or burned. This night was later called *Kristallnacht*—"Crystal Night," or "Night of Broken Glass." That lyrical term, though, softened people's understanding of the shocking brutality of that night, which is more accurately known as the "November Pogroms."

"A Means to an End"

The Nazis created a powerful system of propaganda to mold and manipulate people's beliefs and attitudes. The Nazi government controlled radio stations, theaters, and movie houses, and all the print media. Officials banned books, magazines, and newspapers that promoted ideas they disliked, along with art and music that did not meet with their approval. In response, thousands of artists, scientists, writers, musicians, and professors, both Jewish and non-Jewish, fled the country. Many, however, were arrested or killed.

The Nazis attacked Jews with what Vera Laska, an author and Czech resistance worker, called "an insane whirlwind of hatred lashing out under fancy slogans." For example, propaganda was used to arouse hostility against Jewish businesses. In the August 1938 issue of *Der Stürmer*, a Nazi newspaper,

Julius Streicher used a whole page to attack the 120-year-old business owned by the Israel family in Berlin, a firm that sold furnishings and linens. The business owners were known for honesty and generous treatment of employees, but Streicher claimed that they used "fraud and trickery." The Israels were labeled as "extortioners and exploiters." The article then gave the names and addresses of the company's executives, a not-so-subtle invitation for readers to go after them.

Nazi propaganda disregarded the truth. Josef Goebbels, who directed its operation, once said:

It is beside the point to say your propaganda is too crude, too mean, too brutal, or too unfair, for all this does not matter. . . . Propaganda is always a means to an end.

Fearing for their lives, thousands of Jews packed what little they had left and fled Germany and Austria. Hundreds of thousands more, however, remained. Many thought the worst had passed; others loved their homeland and wanted to stay. By January 1939, the Nazis had a large, well-armed military. The Third Reich had successfully grabbed neighboring Austria and a part of Czechoslovakia called Sudetenland. But Hitler would not stop there. He intended to fulfill a threat that appeared in a 1939 article of a Nazi publication called *Das Schwarze Korps*: The Jews, according to the article, were to be destroyed with "fire and the sword."

"A Long Night of Savagery"

As 1939 began, Jews in Europe had more reason than ever to fear for their lives. Those in Germany and Austria had already experienced Nazi brutality first-hand. Newspapers and radios around the world had reported the savagery of *Kristallnacht*, as witnessed by foreign correspondents, diplomats, and refugees. Men who managed to escape from concentration camps told grim stories of torture and murder. In Italy, anti-Jewish laws had been passed, despite the fact that Italian dictator Benito Mussolini had often said that he himself was not antisemitic.

By 1939, most Jews and anti-Nazis had lost hope of a quick end to Hitler's regime. Tens of thousands of Jews had fled Germany each year beginning in 1935, leaving only perhaps 350,000 of the more than 500,000 who were living in Germany when Hitler rose to power. These were years during which escape was still possible

Soviet foreign commissar Vyacheslav Molotov signs the German–Soviet Non-aggression Pact in August 1939 as Joachim von Ribbentrop and Josef Stalin (center, left and right) look on.

Appeasement and Deceit

On September 29, 1938, Adolf Hitler promised the leaders of France and Great Britain that he would make no more territorial demands if Germany could have Sudetenland, a part of Czechoslovakia. Fearing a war, the French and British appeased him. British prime minister Neville Chamberlain declared that this agreement had brought "peace in our time."

World leaders had taken this same tack in 1935, when Hitler had marched into the Rhineland, a zone between France and Germany that was strictly off limits to Germany under the terms of the Versailles Treaty of 1919.

In 1938, the Allies actually had a chance to stop Hitler once and for all. That August, Ludwig Beck met with several other German generals to express deep concern about Hitler's plan to take Sudetenland. He resigned as chief of the General Staff and formed a group that hoped to overthrow the regime. The group made plans to arrest Hitler and other Nazi officials after the *Führer* ordered an attack on Czechoslovakia. Beck expected a court to convict Hitler on charges of leading Germany into ruin.

To succeed, they needed support from the Western Allies. The men contacted Chamberlain to warn him about the upcoming attack and ask the Allies to stand firm. But the Allies gave Hitler what he wanted without a fight, and the German revolt died.

They appeased him militarily, but world leaders did not unite effectively during the 1930s to stop Nazi persecution of Jews or to give asylum to large numbers of refugees. Hitler concluded that the outside world did not care enough to stop him. He continued his aggression both against other nations and against Jews all over Europe.

and lives could be saved. Nazi policy still focused on driving Jews out, not murdering them, as would happen later.

During the early months of 1939, more Jews tried desperately to escape Nazi persecution. Often, however, they could not find a place to go. Other countries severely restricted the numbers and nationalities of people who could immigrate each year. Without permission to enter another country, many thousands of people found themselves trapped in a nation that wanted them out.

Some Jewish refugees had relatives in other countries who helped them obtain visas by promising to be financially responsible for them once they arrived. Manny Gale's family, ordered to leave

Germany after *Kristallnacht*, had relatives in Virginia who helped them enter the United States. To gain their freedom, the Gales had to pay large bribes to Nazi officials. They endured a difficult ocean journey and were briefly imprisoned in Cuba before they reached America in March 1939. Later, Manny Gale served with the 100th Infantry Division Intelligence Staff of the U.S. Army Air Corps during the war.

The Gales were among the lucky few. Most Jews lacked enough money to bribe officials and had no friends or relatives to help. The less fortunate lined up by the hundreds each day outside the offices of foreign embassies, forced to rely on these governments for help. In general, however, these governments showed little willingness to help.

Czechoslovakia Falls to the Reich

In March, as the Gale family landed an ocean away from the Nazis, the situations of other Jewish refugees became increasingly desperate. Hitler's troops were prepared to move again, this time heading for Czechoslovakia.

The previous September, Hitler had seized one-fifth of this nation when he took the Sudetenland region. Czech president Edvard Benes had left the country and set up a government-in-exile in England. Hitler helped to install a new government in Czecho-slovakia with an elderly, mild-mannered president, Dr. Emil Hacha.

Hitler had often boasted that he would wipe Czechoslovakia "off the map." Using the kinds of tactics that had divided people in Germany, Nazi leaders worked to arouse antagonism between the Czechs and Slovaks, the two major ethnic groups there.

"Let Us Not Lose Our Heads"

The Nazis' anti-Jewish propaganda failed to gain widespread support in Czechoslovakia. When that country was formed in 1918, Jews had attained greater rights of citizenship than in many other countries. They had appreciated the chance to pursue edu-cation and to enter various professions.

As was true with the German Jews, the Czech Jews were proud of their cultured and distinguished heritage, which dated back centuries. A Czech war-veterans group was among those who spoke out against Nazi tactics. They warned their countrymen: "Let us not lose our heads. Antisemitism is not in the interest of the Czech nation."

Unable to persuade the Czech masses to his way of thinking, Hitler resorted to force. On March 14, 1939, he met with President Hacha in Berlin. The Czech leader was shocked to encounter a loud, belligerent Hitler who accused the Czechs of committing wrongful acts against Germany. The *Führer* announced that his troops had orders to invade Czechoslovakia and would behave ruthlessly unless Hacha signed a statement of surrender that directed the Czechs not to resist them.

Hacha refused. For several hours, German officials harassed him, threatening to bomb Prague, the Czech capital. At one point, Hacha fainted, but he finally signed the documents.

German tanks rolled into Czechoslovakia on the morning of March 15, 1939. Freedom-loving Czechs cringed; many people wept openly. Lisa Liebschutz Rosza, a Czech Jew who eventually escaped, later recalled those grim days: "Germans had torn down the street signs and replaced them with German names. Huge swastikas hung like dirty linen over the buildings."

Hitler's latest aggression roused protest around the world. In New York City, a group of 20,000 people marched in a public protest called "Stop Hitler." About 500,000 came out to support the marchers.

The British government—temporarily placated by Hitler's promises of nonaggression—realized that the *Führer* had flagrantly lied. It was now clear that Germany was bent on nothing less than world domination. In an angry speech, British prime minister Neville Chamberlain denounced the German leader. Two weeks later, he pledged that Great Britain would honor its alliance with Poland and defend that country. France also publicly renewed its ties with Poland.

Violence Flares

Meanwhile, Nazism began to engulf the Jews of Czechoslovakia. In the document of surrender that he had forced Hacha to sign, Hitler declared that the Germans would restore "calm, order and peace" in the region and "take the Czech people under the protection of the Third Reich." In reality, however, this new conquest merely provided the Germans with more territory and more victims for their systematic programs of persecution. As American journalist William Shirer wrote: "For the Czechs a long night of German savagery now settled over their land."

With the fall of Czechoslovakia, approximately 120,000 Jews found themselves under Hitler's thumb. As they had done elsewhere, the Germans methodically passed highly restrictive laws against Jews and began seizing their property.

Violence flared as the invaders burned down synagogues and looted Jewish shops and businesses. In one town, Nazis started burning a Jewish home for the poor. Angry Czechs worked to put out the fire and took turns guarding the home before they were overpowered by armed Nazis. Non-Jewish (Gentile) Czechs also showed their support by continuing to shop in Jewish-owned stores after the Nazis required these places to display an important Jewish symbol, the six-pointed Star of David.

In July, Adolf Eichmann arrived in Prague. A high-ranking Nazi officer, Eichmann was known for his harsh treatment of Jews in Vienna, where he had headed the department of Jewish emigration. He now became the director of emigration in Czechoslovakia. Immediately, Eichmann ordered that 70,000 Jews must leave within a year. Unless a specified number of emigrants left each week, he threatened, the same number of people would be sent to concentration camps.

A *Judenrat* ("Jewish Council") was set up to carry out Eichmann's orders and to keep him informed about the number of Jews who left. The Council was also expected to provide the funds people needed for transportation and travel documents—yet there was no money to do so.

Closed Doors

People fleeing from Nazi persecution had few choices. At the time, Shanghai, in China, was the only place that could be entered without legal permission. By the end of 1939, thousands of Jews had found asylum there. But Shanghai had become overcrowded, and some residents were showing hostility toward newcomers.

Between 1933 and 1939, about 100,000 Jewish refugees went to the United States. Another 150,000 went to various European nations that had not yet been occupied by Germany—England, France, Holland, Belgium, Switzerland.

Of the approximately 40,000 who went to Latin America, about half went to Argentina. Most countries in the region, however, closed the door to more refugees at the end of 1938, just when the need became most pressing.

Earlier that year, a conference had been held in Evian, France, for the purpose of discussing refugees. The Jews of Europe felt hopeful, knowing that U.S. president Franklin D. Roosevelt, leader of a great democracy, had initiated the conference. The meeting drew representatives from 32 nations. Some of those countries had vast areas of unpopulated land—for example, Australia, Brazil, and Canada. But, of the 32 nations, only the Dominican Republic dramatically changed its policies or offered to extend help to the refugees. Even the United States, which sponsored the meeting, did not propose a plan of action. Holland and Denmark continued to offer asylum, but these small nations were already crowded.

Throughout 1939, the doors to most countries remained shut to Jewish refugees—especially poor ones. Other factors also prevented people from finding asylum. Around the world, nations were still reeling from the Great Depression, which had caused widespread poverty and left millions without jobs. The United States and other countries had existing laws that set rigid quota systems for immigrants. In addition to all these barriers, refugees who petitioned for help encountered indifference as well as the ugly problem of antisemitism.

The Debate in America

American Jews did not agree on what should be done about the refugee crisis. Some worried that large numbers of Jewish refugees would heighten antisemitism. People who worked to increase quotas for immigrants, including members of the Roosevelt administration, faced powerful opposition from Congress. Some politicians did not want any more immigrants, period; others did not want Jewish refugees in particular.

Immigration and the British

The Jews of the Middle Eastern land of Palestine, however, were eager to welcome any number of refugees. To them, part of Palestine was *Eretz Israel*, their "ancestral homeland," a place where they could build a secure Jewish state. But the British had governed Palestine since 1922 (and would continue to do so until 1948). Each month, the British government issued only 817 "Certificates of Entry" for Jews to come to Palestine legally. This was fewer than 10,000 a year.

In May 1939, the British government issued its "White Paper," a document regarding Jewish immigration to Palestine. Through the Balfour Declaration of 1917, the British had said that Palestine should become a "national home" for the Jewish people. In a turnabout, they now announced: "His Majesty's government now declares that it is not part of their policy that Palestine should become a Jewish state."

The White Paper stated that Jewish refugees would be allowed to enter Palestine only for the next five years, at a rate of just 10,000 per year. The government did agree to admit 25,000 at once if they could show they would not pose any economic burden. Only 70,000 Jews managed to get to Palestine by 1941—after which time escape from Europe was not possible.

Among the British politicians who urged more immigration permits for Jewish refugees was Winston Churchill, then a powerful member of Parliament. But despite his eloquent speeches, Churchill was outvoted and ignored.

Turned Away: The S.S. *St. Louis*

Throughout 1939 and 1940, desperate Jewish refugees tried to escape Europe by sea. Arranging such a trip was both difficult and expensive. It required a boat capable of withstanding a long voyage as well as a qualified captain and crew to sail it. Adequate supplies and travel documents for all the passengers were other vital necessities.

Some of these ships had no clear destination. Others were so old and run-down that they never reached port.

In May 1939, a total of 930 Jewish refugees boarded the ocean liner S.S. *St. Louis* at the port of Hamburg, Germany. With mixed feelings of deep sorrow, relief, anger, and exultation, they watched the German shoreline disappear as the ship began its journey. They sailed southwest toward Havana,

Cuba; each passenger had paid $150 for landing permits signed by Colonel Manuel Benites, the director general of Cuban Immigration.

When the *St. Louis* reached the port of Havana on May 27, exultation turned to anguish: The Cuban government turned them away. A week before—and perhaps even before the ship set sail—Cuban officials had decided to invalidate the landing permits. It seems they had been pressured by antisemitic citizens, people at the German Embassy, and Cuban workers who feared that the newcomers would take away their jobs.

The U.S. State Department and the American Jewish Joint Distribution Committee negotiated with Cuban president Federico Laredo Brú on behalf of the refugees. The committee offered to

By 1939, the British government feared that war with Hitler and the Axis powers was imminent. With war would come an increased need for Arab oil. The Arabs, however, opposed the presence of a large Jewish population or Jewish state in the Middle East.

Thus, as a result of inaction and a lack of meaningful help from Great Britain and the rest of the world community, millions of Jews were doomed to remain in the midst of persecution and war.

Inge Auerbacher, whose family had lived for generations in southern Germany, was one of those forced to stay in Hitler's Europe. In her book *I Am a Star*, Auerbacher recalled:

pay an additional $500 bond for each passenger. The Cubans countered with a demand for $350,000.

As it became clear that the refugees had no hope of entering Cuba, they petitioned the U.S. State Department and President Franklin D. Roosevelt to let them enter the United States. There was no response. Nearby was the state of Florida, but patrol boats from the U.S. Coast Guard were told to make sure the ship did not land.

In June, the *St. Louis* refugees were forced to turn back. After a five-week ordeal at sea, they reached Antwerp, Belgium. Their joy in finally finding asylum was dampened by the presence of Nazis.

Belgium was one of four countries that had agreed to give entry permits to the people from the *St. Louis,* the others being France, Holland, and Great Britain. Although these countries were still free in 1939, all but the latter would eventually be occupied by Germany. Only those *St. Louis* refugees entering Britain were to remain free throughout the Holocaust. Most of the others would be murdered.

Jewish refugees trapped aboard the *St. Louis* stare out at the dock in Havana Harbor in May 1939. By June, the ship was forced to turn back.

In May 1939, we packed our belongings and sold our house. We left our village and moved in with my grandparents in Jebenhausen. This was to be a short stay, since we still hoped to find a way of leaving Germany. Grandpa soon succumbed to a broken heart. He died from a combination of illness and a disappointment in the country he loved.

The Auerbachers never managed to emigrate. Late in 1941, Inge stood at a train station, waving goodbye to her grandmother and many of her classmates, who were being deported north to Latvia, a German-occupied Soviet republic. She wrote:

I would never see her again. Almost all of these unfortunate people became victims of [killing squads] in a forest near Riga [the Latvian capital]. They had to dig their own graves before they were shot.

Auerbacher and her parents were sent to Theresienstadt, a concentration camp in German-occupied Czechoslovakia, in 1942. She would be one of only about 100 children to survive the camp, out of thousands.

Forced to Prague

On August 11, 1939, all Jews remaining in Czechoslovakia were forced to leave their homes and move to Prague. From there, they would later be deported to camps in Poland at the rate of 200 a day—a total of 45,000 by the end of 1941.

Lisa Liebschutz Rosza managed to avoid this fate by obtaining a visa to Iraq, where her Hungarian-born fiancé was working as an architect. At the British Consulate in Prague, she saw thousands of other Jews pleading for emigration papers. Her precious visa allowed her to board a train that would take her to Genoa, Italy. Throughout that trip, and on a ship from Genoa to Lebanon, Rozsa was interrogated by a woman who had been sent by the Gestapo.

Even in Iraq there was no escaping the Nazis. After a few months of calm, Rashid Ali, a Nazi sympathizer, was appointed prime minister. Ali and Hitler had struck a deal: Hitler would give Iraq weapons—and, later, Palestine, which Hitler expected to conquer. For his part, Ali was to overthrow the royal family of Iraq and defeat the British forces stationed there. Fighting in Iraq soon broke out. Jews were forced to hide or flee until the British had secured their military air base.

Doomed

The numbers of the doomed soon increased—literally by the millions. In August 1939, Hitler signed a non-aggression pact with the Soviet Union. Although he had repeatedly expressed contempt for its Communist government, he needed to have this agreement

Other nations were learning more about the Nazi menace. In the United States, hundreds of European scientists had found refuge from persecution. Among the Jewish refugees were the German-born Albert Einstein and Hungarian Leo Szilard. In August 1939, Szilard and Einstein heard alarming news from Europe: German scientists were trying to split the atom. Such research could lead to the creation of potent nuclear bombs.

Previously a professor of science in Berlin, Albert Einstein resigned his post after the Nazi takeover. He is shown here near the campus of Princeton University in New Jersey, where he accepted a professorship.

funding for a top-secret research effort, called the Manhattan Project, to build an atomic bomb. Refugee scientists played key roles in the project. Hitler's policies of hatred and oppression thus enabled the Allies to amass the greatest scientific brainpool in history. Through their work, these scientists hoped to defeat Hitler and all that he stood for.

As Germany pursued its aggression and Japan plundered the Far East, Roosevelt foresaw disaster.

The two scientists wrote a letter to the American president Franklin D. Roosevelt. It was personally delivered to him in October by his friend Alexander Sachs. After reading and discussing the letter with Sachs, Roosevelt said, "Alex, what you are after is to see that the Nazis don't blow us up." After this meeting, the president authorized

Yet most Americans wanted to avoid involvement in any more European wars. Roosevelt tried to change the isolationist attitudes that prevailed among the American public and in Congress. It would take nearly a year before America would even begin shipping large amounts of war materiel to the Allies.

in place. In it, the Soviets and Germans pledged to remain militarily neutral toward each other.

The success of Hitler's next conquest depended on it. He was ready to attack Poland, a nation he despised—a nation filled with people, including non-Jews, whom he deemed suitable only for slavery. Upon his conquest there, approximately 2 million Polish Jews would find themselves under Hitler's thumb. More than 1 million others would be in territories under Soviet control.

"Close Your Eyes to Pity!"

Late in August 1939, thousands of German armored tanks stood on the alert in East Prussia, Czechoslovakia, and a region called Pomerania. German naval vessels were in position, and the *Luftwaffe*— German Air Force—was ready to move. On August 31, acting on Hitler's orders, SS men disguised in Polish uniforms blew up the German radio station in Gleiwitz, Poland. This carefully planned incident was meant to enrage the German people and provide an excuse for the attack on Poland.

On the eve of this invasion, Hitler spoke to his generals for several hours. He said that Great Britain and France would probably not come to Poland's aid. Even if they did, Hitler assured them, it would be a brief war. The Allies were both weak and

----

German troops open a Polish border gate at the beginning of the invasion, September 1, 1939.

unprepared, and they lacked leaders who were as capable as he and Benito Mussolini of Italy. Raising his voice, Hitler finished his speech with these words:

> *Close your eyes to pity! Act brutally! Eighty million people [the population of Greater Germany] must obtain what is their right! The stronger man is right! Be harsh and remorseless!*

"Lightning War"

On September 1, 1939, German troops entered Poland and quickly overwhelmed its military. Hitler called this strategy a *blitzkrieg,* or "lightning war." He crippled Poland's air power by bombing airfields early on the first day. Jewish civilians were among the first casualties as bombs hit the airfield and nearby Jewish ghetto in Radom, in central Poland.

The Germans proceeded to decimate Poland, attacking from all sides with amazing speed. The Poles were taken by surprise, and terribly outnumbered. A total of 1.5 million German troops advanced on only 500,000 Polish soldiers. The Germans had superior equipment, including self-propelled artillery. They used 2,700 panzers—tanks that could roll across the rough, muddy countryside. The Polish cavalry and foot soldiers fought valiantly, but their lances were no match for powerful tanks.

"Evil Things"

On September 3, France and Great Britain declared war on Germany. They could no longer ignore the threat Hitler posed to all of Europe. British prime minister Neville Chamberlain addressed people by radio, saying, "It is evil things we shall be fighting against, brute force, bad faith, injustice, oppression, and persecution. But against them I am certain that the right shall prevail." World War II had officially begun.

By mid-September, leaders of the Polish government had fled to France. Within a few days, most of Poland had fallen. Only troops in Warsaw kept fighting. Led by their mayor, citizens of all

Approximately 3.3 million Jews lived in Poland before the German invasion of western Poland and the subsequent Soviet invasion of eastern Poland. Centuries of harsh antisemitism had forced these people to rely a great deal on their own resources.

At times during the Middle Ages, when Jews were not allowed to own land or enter most professions, landowners hired Jews to serve as their merchants, moneylenders, and tax collectors. As they carried out these orders, Jews aroused the anger of the lower classes. There was a widespread mistrust of ethnic minorities in general, but feelings toward the Jews always seemed to be the most negative. The Catholic Church fortified its powerful position by exploiting these prejudices and criticizing Jews and their faith.

As social and cultural "outcasts," Polish Jews developed their own vibrant communities. In rural areas, their villages were called *shtetls,* a word from Yiddish, their language. In general, these Polish Jews were traditional people who adhered to old Jewish customs regarding clothing and appearance and who put their faith and religion at the center of their lives. All men were expected to learn how to read, so education flourished in these communities, as did theaters and newspapers.

Carl Hamada, who lived in Frysztak, Poland, before the war, recalled of that *shtetl,* "It was a close community and very poor. People worked in small stores or went to other towns and sold there on market day. On Jewish holidays, our town closed up."

Compared to Jews living in most of Western Europe, Polish Jews mingled less with the Christian population. The majority of Jews in Poland remained separate in dress and custom. As a result, they were often easy to distinguish from non-Jews, which made them that much more vulnerable targets when the Germans moved in.

ages built walls and roadblocks and set German tanks ablaze with homemade gasoline bombs. In response, German planes bombed the city mercilessly.

Soviet troops attacked Poland from the east on September 17. Under the terms of the German–Soviet Non-aggression Pact, which they had signed in August, the Soviets would take over eastern Poland and the Baltic nations of Estonia, Latvia, and Lithuania.

German soldiers board a train bound for Poland at the beginning of the invasion. The writing on the train—paraphrased— means "We are going to Poland to give the Jews a thrashing."

"Living Space"

The Poles were also attacked from within by people of German descent who supported the Nazis. Among them were residents of Oswiecim who shot at the Polish infantry. Before the war, Oswiecim had had a Jewish population of about 7,000 to 8,000. The German occupiers renamed this south-central Polish town Auschwitz and built their largest and most notorious concentration and death camps there.

Warsaw, in central Poland, surrendered on September 25, less than a month after the German invasion. The once beautiful city lay in ruins. Nearly 60,000 Poles had been killed, and more than 700,000 had been taken prisoner.

The Nazis moved quickly to exploit the land and its people. As Hitler envisioned it, Poland was to provide the Third Reich with more *Lebensraum,* or "living space." The Poles (mostly Gentiles), whom Hitler had long despised and whom the Nazis viewed as "subhuman," would be used as a source of cheap or slave labor. Jews and their communities were simply to be wiped out.

"No Other God but Germany"

One of Adolf Hitler's long-term plans was to abolish all religion so that people would revere only Nazi leaders and ideals. Hitler had said, "We shall have no other God but Germany."

During the early 1930s, many religious leaders did not strongly oppose Hitler. Some even supported him—many clergy feared Communism, a political ideology that Hitler pledged to combat. As time passed, however, the Nazis chipped away at the foundations of religion. First, they arrested clergy who spoke against them. In 1936, they banned Catholic youth groups and forbade crucifixes in schools. By 1939, they had banned Catholic newspapers and religious processions.

Soon after the German invasion of Poland, the Nazis arrested prominent Polish Catholic priests. Many were sent to the Pastors' Barracks at Dachau, a concentration camp near Munich, Germany. By 1945, more than 2,270 priests and pastors from 19 German-occupied countries had been imprisoned there; most did not survive.

Catholic nuns were also sent to concentration camps. The Nazis eventually killed more than 400 nuns—in one case, a nun was killed for copying an anti-Nazi poem. Many women at the camps also died as a result of starvation, disease, beatings, and rat bites.

One religious group that was persecuted heavily throughout the Nazi era was the Jehovah's Witnesses. Hitler had called them, among other things, a "degenerate race." Witnesses believe that all real authority comes from God and the Bible. Because of their beliefs, they refused to salute the German flag or fight in any wars.

As early as 1933, the Nazis banned Witnesses from gathering for meetings or praying and studying in their meeting halls. In the following years, hundreds of Witnesses were sent to concentration camps for possessing or distributing their literature, which was smuggled into Germany. If parents refused to sign an oath disavowing their religion, their children were taken away to be raised as Nazis. More than 800 children were sent to Nazi-run state homes for this reason.

By 1945, approximately 6,000 Witnesses had been imprisoned and hundreds had been killed. They included Frieda Metzen, a 32-year-old servant who was arrested for spreading news about foreign radio broadcasts. Also murdered was 48-year-old Helene Gotthold, who actively encouraged German men to resist and not to join the army.

Polish priest Piotr Sosnowski stands, seconds before he is executed, in a wooded area near Piasnica, Poland.

Nazification

The process of Nazification began at once. Polish cities were turned into "German" cities with new names, new street signs, and adorned with German flags, slogans, and posters. All around them, Poles heard German being spoken. When people shopped for fuel or food, they had to make their requests in German or they might be denied service or sent to the back of the line.

Groups of armed Nazis took charge of local governments. As they had elsewhere, they created an atmosphere of fear and violence. Stuffhof concentration camp, for example, was set up in Poland on September 2, one day after the invasion began.

The Germans also ousted Poles from certain regions. Hitler decreed that more than 600,000 Poles must be relocated to central Poland, where they would be placed in special areas. He ordered his SS to round up these Poles, along with thousands of Jews and Romani. People were given two hours or less to gather their belongings; then they were evicted from their homes. They were permitted to take little or no money and only up to about 50 pounds (20 kilograms) of food and clothing.

By the end of 1939, entire communities of Jewish Poles had been moved to cities in central Poland. The Nazis deported people by train, packing them into cattle cars without providing food or water. Once the victims reached their destinations, they were jammed into already overcrowded and filthy ghettos, where life was often brutal.

Reporting to the Polish government-in-exile in France, a Catholic resistance leader named Jan Karski said, "Poles are unbelievably depressed, fearful, and in despair. The common people believe that the Antichrist has descended to earth."

The Nazis next began to target Poles who had any power or influence, such as the clergy, professors, and labor-union leaders. Because it was feared that they might cause problems for the new regime, these people were to be killed at once.

Any well-educated Pole was regarded as a threat. High-ranking Nazi Heinrich Himmler called for a ban on education in Poland over fourth grade, figuring that Poles would need little schooling to fulfill their lowly roles in the Third Reich. Himmler said that the Poles need not learn to read; instead they should be taught "the doctrine that it is divine law to obey the Germans."

"We Could Not Walk by a German..."

As soon as German forces reached Poland, the Nazis began terrorizing Jews. Synagogues were burned and Jewish businesses and homes were robbed. Jewish citizens were ordered to give up all their valuables.

Top: As an act of public humiliation, an SS man cuts the beard of a Jew on a street in Warsaw. **Middle:** A group of German police and SS officers cut the sidelocks off the son of a rabbi. **Bottom:** Six Jewish men are publicly humiliated on the streets of Warsaw—they are ordered to do "gymnastics" for the camera.

Gestapo units enforced numerous anti-Jewish laws. Jews, for example, were forbidden to hold any meetings or religious services. They could not walk on the sidewalks. They could not shop or use public transportation during certain hours. Jews were banned from owning radios or telephones; public telephones were also declared off limits. David Eiger, who lived in Radom at the time, recalled:

We could not walk by a German with our hat on; we had to take off the hat and greet the German. . . . You could not be found outside without a permit. And all this was under the penalty of death. The Germans would just shoot, no questions asked.

The violence against the Polish Jews knew no bounds. Nazis harassed and beat them on the streets and urged other Poles to join in; some people used Jews for target practice. In one town, approximately 50 Jews were taken into a synagogue and shot. On harsh winter days, Nazis ordered groups of Jews outside and sprayed them with icy water.

Jews and other Poles were regularly seized at random and forced to work as slaves. By then, slave-labor camps were being run for many purposes. Captives were worked to exhaustion—and often to death—digging ditches, constructing walls, carrying rocks, and doing other backbreaking jobs. In Lodz, a city in central Poland, slave laborers made clothing and other war supplies for Germany. The guards shot those who tried to escape.

"A Chance to Be Reborn"

One German officer explained that committing brutal acts was not only effective, but also that those acts

. . . make men of us, they make us aware of our position as the Master Race. The Czechs, Slovaks, and Poles offer us a chance to be reborn, to become the grand, old, barbaric, forceful Germany, free of the smallness and weakness of soft cultures and Jewish Christianity.

As in other countries, most Poles were passive bystanders to the persecution of the Jews. An active minority joined or assisted the Nazis. Antisemitism had deep roots in Poland, and the Nazis found many people to help them. The occupation also benefited those Poles who were able to acquire Jewish businesses and property. The Nazis offered money and various goods—sugar, salt, cigarettes, extra food—to people who informed on Jews. Gangs tracked down Jews who were hiding and demanded money as a bribe for not exposing them or their protectors.

Strong Polish resistance groups were forming, however, and Nazis received less help from the Polish police, who were generally uncooperative. According to historian Raul Hilberg, "Of all the native police forces in occupied Eastern Europe, those of Poland were least involved in anti-Jewish actions."

Marking the Jews

It was in Poland that Jews were first made to wear yellow cloth symbols that classified them by religion. On October 24, Jews in Wloclawek, who numbered about 10,000, were ordered to wear large yellow triangles on their clothing. Within a month, all Jews in Poland had to wear a mark of some kind—a yellow patch or star, or a white armband with the Star of David—bearing the word *Jude* ("Jew"). As a further insult, they had to pay for these items themselves.

The labels were meant to be a mark of shame, since the Nazis called Jews the "eternal enemy" of humankind. Jews knew that they had no reason to feel ashamed, but this public humiliation also made them ready targets for violence. In effect, Jews had been branded for all to see—clearly marked for the Nazis and their helpers.

The Allies Respond

Having declared war against Germany, the Allied nations prepared for attacks. Air-raid shelters were quickly built, and gas masks were distributed to citizens. Millions of people were evac-

Der Distriktschef von Krakau

ANORDNUNG

Kennzeichnung der Juden im Distrikt Krakau

Ich ordne an, dass alle Juden im Alter von über 12 Jahren im Distrikt Krakau mit Wirkung vom 1. 12. 1939 ausserhalb ihrer eigenen Wohnung ein sichtbares Kennzeichen zu tragen haben. Dieser Anordnung unterliegen auch nur vorübergehend im Distriktsbereich anwesende Juden für die Dauer ihres Aufenthaltes.

Als Jude im Sinne dieser Anordnung gilt:

1. wer der mosaischen Glaubensgemeinschaft angehört oder angehört hat,
2. jeder, dessen Vater oder Mutter der mosaischen Glaubensgemeinschaft angehört oder angehört hat.

Als Kennzeichen ist am rechten Oberarm der Kleidung und der Überkleidung eine Armbinde zu tragen, die auf weissem Grunde an der Aussenseite einen blauen Zionstern zeigt. Der weisse Grund muss eine Breite von mindestens 10 cm. haben, der Zionstern muss so gross sein, dass dessen gegenüberliegende Spitzen mindestens 8 cm. entfernt sind. Der Balken muss 1 cm. breit sein.

Juden, die dieser Verpflichtung nicht nachkommen, haben strenge Bestrafung zu gewärtigen.

Für die Ausführung dieser Anordnung, insbesondere die Versorgung der Juden mit Kennzeichen, sind die Ältestenräte verantwortlich.

Krakau, den 18. 11. 1939.

Dr. **Wächter**
Gouverneur

Szef dystryktu krakowskiego

ROZPORZĄDZENIE

Znamionowanie żydów w okręgu Krakowa

Zarządzam z ważnością od dnia 1. XII. 1939, iż wszyscy żydzi w wieku ponad 12 lat winni nosić widoczne znamiona. Rozporządzeniu temu podlegają także na czas ich pobytu przejściowo w obrębie okręgu przebywający żydzi.

Żydem w myśl tego rozporządzenia jest:

1) ten, który jest lub był wyznania mojżeszowego,
2) każdy, którego ojciec, lub matka są lub byli wyznania mojżeszowego.

Znamieniem jest biała przepaska noszona na prawym rekawie ubrania lub odzienia wierzchniego z niebieską gwiazdą sjonistyczną. Przepaska winna mieć szerokość conajmniej 10 cm, a gwiazda średnicę 8 cm. Wstążka, z której sporządzono gwiazdę, winna mieć szerokość conajmniej 1 cm.

Niestosujący się do tego zarządzenia zostaną surowo ukarani.

Za wykonanie niniejszego zarządzenia, zwłaszcza za dostarczenie opasek cz... ...powiedzialna Rada starszych.

Kraków, dnia 18. XI. 1939.

(—) **Wächter**
Gubernator

This announcement—posted in Cracow in November 1939—ordered all Jews above the age of 12 to wear an armband with the Star of David.

uated from London and other large British cities. No British troops went to Poland, however. To get there, they would have had to cross German soil, and Poland was already completely lost.

The "Jewish Question"

Heinrich Himmler, the head of the SS—*Schutzstaffel*—a group of Nazi police organizations including the Gestapo, reorganized the Reich Security Main Office. He put Heinrich Müller in charge of the Gestapo, whose job it was to get rid of "enemies of the Reich." Adolf Eichmann was assigned to handle the evacuation of Jews in all occupied areas. Hitler and his top aides talked at length about what they referred to as the "Jewish question" or "problem."

By the end of 1939, Reinhard Heydrich had laid out the Nazi plans for Jews in occupied Poland: They would be gathered together, registered, and then evacuated to ghettos. A Jewish Council made up of Jews would be set up in each ghetto to carry out SS orders. During the fall, a ghetto was established in Piotrkow Trybunalski; other ghettos were taking shape.

Heydrich, whom Hitler called the "Man with the Iron Heart," also mentioned a second stage of their operations: the "final aim." He said that this final goal would take time and "must be kept strictly secret." This goal was inspired by the fact that elimination of European Jewry was not moving fast enough to suit the Nazis. They felt that new, more brutal methods were called for.

Little documentation or detail about these discussions has ever come to light. The men who were later to implement this "Final Solution to the Jewish question" knew that their plans were so extreme that no one should speak of it publicly or put it in writing.

"The Soil Bleeds"

As the new decade of the 1940s dawned, the Nazis seemed invincible. Hitler was busy developing new military exploits to give Germany more power and resources. The Nazis also continued their plans to eliminate people who did not fit into what they called their "master race." They built death centers and pondered new methods for "cleansing" or "purifying" the Reich of those they called *Untermenschen*—"subhumans." While the Nazis continued to terrorize a ravaged Poland, members of the Polish resistance sang a song with these words: "When a German puts his foot down, the soil bleeds a hundred years."

"Special Duty" Squads

To help implement their program of intimidation and elimination, the Nazis formed groups of specially trained SS men to take on a murderous new role. These strike-force groups were called *Einsatzgruppen*—"Special Duty Squads."

A starving woman stands with two children in front of a closed shop in the Warsaw ghetto.

Toward a "Master Race"

According to Hitler, numerous groups of people—many of them Aryans—were deemed useless. They included people with mental or physical disabilities, those with epilepsy or an incurable illness, and those who were senile, deformed, or too sickly to work.

To preserve their "master race," the Nazis banned people with hereditary diseases from marrying. The Law for the Prevention of Offspring with Hereditary Defects, which had been passed in 1933, required people with certain conditions, such as deafness, to be sterilized so that they could not have children. A special tribunal decided who would be sterilized, and victims had no choice in the matter. Those who tried to avoid the surgery were hunted down, their families harassed. By 1939, about 400,000 people in Germany had been sterilized.

By that time, however, the Nazis had concluded that sterilization was a slow way to attain their goals. Hitler saw no reason to house and feed people who could not serve his war effort. In October 1939, he approved the T-4 Program, which legalized so-called euthanasia, the "mercy killings" of mentally and physically disabled people. In the meantime, mental patients were being neglected and given so little food that many died of starvation or physical illnesses.

Six extermination centers were built in "Greater Germany." They were staffed

Einsatzgruppen had already been used in 1938 in annexed Austria. There, the men in these groups had apprehended people who opposed the Reich. Later, they had followed the invading German Army into Czechoslovakia to handle matters relating to "the national economy."

In the fall of 1939, there were six squads, made up of about 2,000 men. As the Germans conquered Poland, the SS were told to round up Jews for "resettlement" in cities. They were also authorized to kill civilians. Reinhard Heydrich described their task as "the housecleaning of Jews, intelligentsia, clergy, and the nobility."

Before killing, the squads first took civilians to remote areas. There, victims were often forced to dig their own graves before they were shot. The *Einsatzgruppen* moved ruthlessly from one German-occupied Polish town to another. They would later repeat these horrors on an even larger scale in Lithuania, Latvia, the Soviet Union, and elsewhere.

by specially trained members of the SS. People were sent to these centers in special buses with painted windows that blocked anyone from seeing in or out. Once they arrived, people were killed in a highly efficient, methodical way. Staff members either administered deadly injections or sent arrivals to a "shower" that was really lethal gas.

Soon Hitler approved the use of gas to kill mental patients, Jews, and others. A number of death centers now tried this out. Inside airtight rooms, victims sat on wooden benches as poison gas was piped in. Death was both painful and prolonged, taking 10 to 15 terrifying minutes. The victims' bodies were then burned in crematoria, huge ovens built expressly for this purpose.

Families received the victims' ashes in the mail, along with letters informing them that their relatives had died "during surgery" or from an "illness." Though victims' families were advised not to ask questions, they grew suspicious. When the truth emerged, Catholic leaders and others protested the T-4 Program. But by then, an estimated 60,000 to 93,000 people had been killed in this way. The Nazis had also had a chance to test certain experimental methods that they would later use to murder millions in the death camps. And, though the program officially ended on September 1, 1941, this kind of killing continued even after the war.

"Death Boxes"

On December 16, 1939, *The Times* of London published an article under the headline "A Stony Road to Extermination." It reported that Germany planned to force more than 1 million people from Germany, Austria, Czechoslovakia, and Poland to move to an area near Lublin, Poland, that was set up as a "Jewish reserve." Soon, however, the plan was dropped. The Germans were not equipped to carry it out at that time, and they disliked the criticism they were receiving in the world press.

Instead, the Nazis worked to concentrate all Jews within urban areas and ghettos that had access to railroad lines. This measure was what Heydrich had outlined back in September, when he said that Jews were to be kept in place while the Nazis prepared for the elimination of European Jewry.

By February 1940, a ghetto was being formed in Lodz, Poland, where about 200,000 Jews had lived before the war. The Lodz

Allowed only to bring what would fit in a cart, Jews in Cracow, Poland, wheel their belongings into the ghetto.

ghetto was completed on May 1, and 160,000 Jews were sealed inside its walls. A few days earlier, Nazi officials had ordered a large concentration camp to be built near Auschwitz in Poland.

The largest ghetto was in Warsaw. About 400,000 Jews had lived there before 1939, giving Warsaw the largest Jewish population of any city. The Warsaw ghetto covered 100 square blocks, surrounded by barbed wire. Non-Jews were moved out, and all Jews were ordered inside. In addition to the hundreds of thousands already there, tens of thousands were brought to the ghetto from rural Poland.

When the Jews were sent to the ghetto, an eyewitness observed how people moved along the streets "in an endless stream . . . "

> . . . pushing, wheeling, dragging all their belongings from every part of the city to one small section. . . . They could bring very little, only what would fit in their arms or on a cart. The Nazis had forbidden them to use cars or horses. Some onlookers amused themselves by knocking over the carts and watching the desperate owners struggle to retrieve their belongings.

Inside the ghetto, there was terrible confusion as people scrambled to find housing. The ghetto contained only 2.5 percent of the land area in Warsaw, but these hundreds of thousands of people exceeded one-third of the city's population. Every room was soon filled, yet more people kept coming. Many families shared one small apartment, ranging from 6 to 14 people in each room.

The Nazis ran the ghettos with brute force. Laws kept people isolated and prevented them from obtaining enough food, medicine, and other supplies. A Jewish Council was formed in every ghetto to carry out the Nazis' orders. The *Judenrat* members were under great strain and pressure. If they did not perform as instructed, the Nazis would punish the entire community. They would also replace uncooperative members with someone else.

Walled In

In the early months, Warsaw Jews could still go outside the confines of the ghetto to work or to perform specific tasks. Those with jobs had a better chance of survival, since they might have access to food. But construction of high red brick walls began in the summer of 1940. Soon residents found themselves locked up behind guarded gates. The penalty for leaving illegally was death. People in the Cracow ghetto were

Jews entering the Lodz ghetto, March 1940.

A boy who has fainted from hunger lies on the sidewalk in the Lodz ghetto.

also imprisoned, behind walls made to mimic Jewish tombstones.

The ghettos soon became known as "death boxes." Given the terrible conditions, the Nazis predicted that hunger and disease alone would kill many Jews. According to one source, under German domination, non-ghettoized Poles were allowed only 800 calories a day—less than half of what a typical slim adult requires to maintain the same weight. The rations for Jews in the ghettos were even less. Eventually, their rations would sink to under 200 calories a day, in the form of a little bread, sugar, and fat.

Lacking protein and vitamins, people literally wasted away. They suffered from scurvy and other diseases caused by malnutrition. With serious vitamin deficiencies, many lost their ability to fight off illness. Crowding and a lack of sanitation and clean water caused diseases to spread rapidly. It was not long before ghetto residents began collapsing on the street. Hirsh Altusky, a survivor of the Warsaw ghetto, later recalled, "Every day when you walked out of the house, you saw dead bodies, skin and bones covered with newspaper."

In order to survive, people smuggled food, which they often shared with others. Many smugglers were children. They were the only ones small enough to crawl through cracks in the walls or under fences. People were also more likely to help a starving child than an adult.

Hunger made people desperate enough to risk death, which became the punishment for smuggling. Some German guards took bribes as payment for overlooking smuggling activities. Other guards would shoot anyone they caught, often on the spot. One guard at the Lodz ghetto filed a report describing how he shot a woman as she reached through the ghetto fence to take some turnips from a passing cart: "I made use of my firearm. The Jewess received 2 fatal shots. . . . Signed, Sergeant Naumann." At other times, guards hung people publicly as a warning to others.

By 1940, many free citizens of Warsaw knew that Jews were being murdered and brutalized behind the ghetto's walls. They had seen the piles of coffins being carted off and heard children behind the wall begging for food. One non-Jewish Pole recalled, "In 1940, as they transported Jews to the ghetto, I lived near the ghetto and saw people begging for bread. I saw them finished off." Another said:

> In 1940 the Germans caught a Jew who had escaped from the ghetto, and they told him to put smoking cigars inside his mouth. They were laughing at him. We could hear the Jew screaming.

Despite the appalling conditions, residents still tried to function as a community. They even set up schools and makeshift hospitals. Jewish religious services, outlawed by the Nazis, were held in secret. Creative ghetto-dwellers found various ways to perform

Cracow ghetto residents chop up furniture for use as fuel, 1940.

The Nazis did not hesitate to try new killing methods on children. In 1940, a group of 250 Romani children from Brno, Czechoslovakia, were taken from their families and sent to an extermination center in Germany. They were murdered with a gas called Zyklon B. Nazi scientists wanted to test the "efficiency" of this new poison.

Along with Jews, the Romani were targeted for destruction by the Nazis. These people, from two tribal groups called Roma and Sinti, had come to Europe from India in the 1300s, spreading both east and west. Like Jews, they had been persecuted for centuries and banned from joining craftsmen's guilds that would enable them to get jobs. Unlike the Jews, most Romani could not

A group of Romani prisoners awaits further instruction at Belzec concentration camp, 1941.

read and write. They became talented musicians, armormakers, weavers, basketmakers, jewelers, and horse-breeders.

The Romani were often outcast because of prejudice against their dark skin color and some of their customs, such as fortune-telling. In certain countries, rewards were given to those who brought in a Romani, dead or alive, to the local authorities.

In 1899, Germany set up its "Central Office for Fighting the Gypsy Menace." During the 1920s, all Romani were required to be registered, photographed, and fingerprinted. The Nuremberg criteria and definitions were applied to Romani as well as Jews. The laws defined "Gypsies" as people who had at least two Romani great-grandparents out of eight. The Nazis claimed such people had "evil blood" with criminal tendencies.

Three mass arrests of Romani took place, in 1939, 1941, and 1943. The first arrests were in Germany and Austria. More followed in Poland, Yugoslavia, and Czechoslovakia, then Hungary, Romania, and Bulgaria. While imprisoned in concentration camps, Romani were also sterilized without anesthesia and subjected to brutal "medical experiments." Estimates vary, but it is believed that perhaps as many as 200,000 Romani were murdered during the Holocaust. Thousands of others were tortured, scarred, and physically debilitated.

Two workers sit with a burial wagon on the streets of the Warsaw ghetto, 1941. Covered wagons such as this were eventually replaced by crude, open wooden carts.

theatrical and musical productions, and some wrote poetry and other literature. Ghetto diarist Chaim Kaplan described the spirit and strength of the Jews around him:

> *They love life and they do not wish to disappear from the earth before their time. . . . As long as this secret power is still within us, we do not give up any hope.*

Cut off from the outside world, ghetto residents tried to follow the progress of the war. Most of the news they received during 1940, however, was bleak. Hitler's armies were marching across Europe, defeating one country after another. Meanwhile, the ghetto's people existed from hour to hour, watching and waiting for some sign that things were going to change. One survivor summed up their plight this way: "The devil himself could not have devised such hell."

"We Shall Never Surrender"

While Jews perished in the ghettos of German-occupied Poland, Nazi Germany aimed its military machine at the western front. Although the British and French had declared war on Germany in September 1939, no real fighting had taken place. As a result, people spoke of the "phony war." New Nazi aggression in 1940, however, abruptly ended that state of affairs.

As rumors of an expanding war reached the Warsaw ghetto, Chaim Kaplan wrote in his diary:

The sides are gearing up for a terrible battle whose likes the world has yet to witness. A time of momentous events for each side looms steadily closer, yet the war against Polish Jewry does not let up for a single moment.

A French man weeps as he and others watch German troops march into Paris on June 14, 1940.

A class of Dutch Jewish children—each wearing the mandatory Star of David, circa May 1940.

As German-occupied lands expanded into Western Europe, so did Jewish suffering. Many Jews who had left the Reich only a short time ago—for what had been "safe" countries elsewhere in Europe—would now face the Nazi threat yet again.

Conquests in the North

On the morning of April 9, 1940, the German Army launched a surprise attack on Denmark and Norway. Hitler knew that he must capture these neutral Scandinavian countries before he could invade Great Britain. He planned to place submarine bases on the Norwegian coast and to secure that coastline. It was also along the route taken by ships that hauled iron ore from Sweden to Germany.

The people of Denmark, approximately 8,000 of them Jews, watched in shock as freighters brought German troops to their land. The Danes lacked the arms or troops to protect their democratic nation. The German ambassador told King Christian X that Denmark was now under the Reich's "protection."

In Norway, the navy fired at the Germans from ironclad ships in Narvik harbor. Norwegian fire at the port of Oskarsborg sank one German ship and damaged another; British dive-bombers came to Norway's aid, sinking a German cruiser in Bergen harbor.

From a new location in the mountains, King Haakon VII continued to run the government and to encourage active resistance. But in June, the spirited Norwegians admitted defeat and the king fled to exile in England.

German Occupation Expands

By then, Germany had also attacked three other small, neutral nations without ever declaring war. About 4,500 Jews lived in Luxembourg when the Germans struck there on May 9, 1940. In Belgium, approximately 66,000 Jews became captive prey in the wake of an invasion that began on May 10.

That same day, people in Holland were awakened by gunfire and rumbling noises. Radio announcers declared that German planes had bombed Dutch airfields and munitions dumps. For the next few days, German tanks swarmed into Holland, plowing through hastily built Dutch roadblocks.

The Dutch had not been at war for over a century, so they kept only a small army. Still, they kept fighting, with help from French, British, and Belgian troops. Then, on May 14, German forces destroyed Rotterdam, killing and injuring thousands. Hitler vowed to bomb other cities unless Holland surrendered. By then, Queen Wilhelmina and the Dutch government had left for England.

In Holland, religious tolerance dated back to the 1600s. Jews were an accepted part of every area of Dutch life, and most were solidly middle class. As the Nazis rose to prominence in Europe, no anti-Jewish riots had occurred in Holland. Now, the country's more than 140,000 Jews faced a new threat from outside.

As European countries were invaded, many Jews tried to flee. Some managed to reach France or Portugal, but most were trapped. Harbors were blocked, and mine fields had been placed in the North Sea.

The Prinz family were among those who tried to leave Holland. They told author Leesha Rose what they saw at Ijmuiden harbor, where thousands arrived by car and bicycle in the spring of 1940:

To save people from the Nazis, Jews in Palestine organized sea voyages, conducted in secrecy. In November 1939, a group of 1,500 German and Austrian refugees boarded one of these secret ships. They had come by riverboat down the Danube River to the Black Sea, where they boarded an oil tanker in Kladovo on the coast of Yugoslavia.

The passengers faced many hardships. The weather was bitterly cold, and, for bedding, people had one thin blanket apiece. There was little to eat or drink besides noodles and coffee.

The leader of this trip was 25-year-old Ruth Kluger, a member of an Israeli resistance group called the Mossad. She had grown up in Romania and was living in Palestine when the Mossad invited her to join. She knew nine languages and looked, they said, like "a teen-aged schoolgirl." Kluger and her colleagues asked the Bulgarian government for visas so the passengers could stop at its port, Varna, where the ship *Hulda* would pick them up for the trip to Palestine; the *Hulda* was hidden nearby behind high cliffs at the port of Balchik.

After first sitting at the dock in Kladovo for more than a month, the ship finally left, but with only 727 passengers. Along the way, two British ships spotted the vessel and accompanied it to Palestine. Since the passengers' visas were for Paraguay, the British insisted that the ship go there. When they refused, the passengers were placed in prison camps. Six months later, the British relented and let the refugees become legal residents of Palestine.

Kluger later described the desperate mood of her passengers, who believed they were doomed in Europe. If these people had thought they would still be in danger, she said,

[t]hey would not have fled from their homes, leaving everything behind them. The street they lived on. The school their children went to. The shops they knew. Leaving their friends, their relatives. Leaving their life behind them. For what? To try to reach a homeland they had never seen. Palestine.

Kluger continued to work in and out of Romania to organize more rescue missions. In November 1940, the Iron Guard—Romanian Nazis—took over the country. The king of Romania was removed, and 64 officials were killed.

The Romanian Nazis knew about Kluger and came to arrest her in December. She managed to escape through a bathroom window, and then fled to Turkey. Later, she said:

To keep going, one had to learn not to cry. When it came to what was happening to the Jews—one could not cry. Otherwise one would cry all the time.

*The German planes were circling above the sea and shooting at
the full boats and we saw people falling into the water. . . .*

*People were clamoring impatiently to escape, offering money
and jewelry for a place on a boat. But only a few boats got away.*

Among those trapped in Holland were about 25,000 German
refugees, including Otto and Edith Frank and their daughters
Margot and Anne. Anne Frank, who was 12 years old in 1940,
would later become well-known as the author of a diary that
described her life in hiding during the German occupation. Like
most of the other Dutch Jews, she would not survive the war.

The victorious Germans now headed for France. By May 20,
German tanks had reached Abbeville, on the French coast of the
English Channel. Germany won a decisive battle in northern
Belgium, and thousands of Belgian, British, and French troops
were stranded on beaches around Dunkirk. German armored
columns were ordered to Dunkirk to capture these men.

A Dynamic New Leader

At this point, Hitler believed that the British were finished.
Great Britain, however, now had a new prime minister: Winston
Churchill. For several years, this dynamic leader had been warning the world not to appease the Nazis. With Churchill in charge,
the British became determined to stop Hitler once and for all.

While the Germans pondered their next move, the Allies
conducted a massive rescue effort at Dunkirk. To aid the Royal
Navy, private boats made numerous trips across the English
Channel. The Royal Air Force staved off German fighters long
enough for the boats to save more than 338,000 men.

After the daring rescue, in a famous speech that was heard
by people in many lands, Churchill said:

*Even though large tracts of Europe and many old and famous
states have fallen or may fall into the grip of the Gestapo
and the odious apparatus of Nazi rule, we shall not flag or fail.*

We shall fight in France, we shall fight in the seas and oceans, we shall fight. . . in the air. We shall fight on the landing grounds. We shall fight in the fields and on the streets. We shall never surrender.

The British Expeditionary Forces were already badly in need of munitions and other supplies. They had suffered grave losses and had run out of rifles and other equipment. As determined as they were, the Allies still had several long years of war ahead of them.

Swastikas over France

By the end of May, German forces dominated northern France. They reached Paris on June 14. Almost immediately, a large Nazi flag, with its characteristic swastika, was raised above the Eiffel Tower. France surrendered on June 22 and asked for an armistice (truce). Hitler was elated.

Hitler (center) poses with two fellow Nazis in front of the Eiffel Tower only a week after German forces took Paris.

Great Britain declared that it would continue to fight, despite Hitler's guarantee that Britain would be left alone. The British declaration meant that the war could not end unless Hitler either invaded Britain (a plan the Germans called "Operation Sea Lion") or convinced the British to give up. Hitler opted for a show of force and decided to terrify British civilians with air attacks. For several nights, thousands of bombs hit London and other cities, causing widespread deaths, injuries, and destruction. On September 15, the Germans launched a daytime strike, but they were stopped by the British before reaching London. Many German planes were lost.

Great Britain now seemed out of reach. But Hitler had France.

In 1939, some 300,000 Jews had been living in France (about 1 percent of the population). Some were natives, others were foreign-born. Another 40,000 to 50,000 Jews had come as refugees from Belgium and Holland.

Hitler annexed the Alsace-Lorraine region, which bordered Germany, and divided the fallen nation into two parts, with the north occupied by the Germans and the south declared a "Free Zone." Led by Marshal Petain, the "Vichy government" that controlled the Free Zone cooperated with the Germans in numerous ways. One prominent Vichy official was a well-known Nazi.

Because France bordered neutral Switzerland, Spain, and Italy—and had many ports—many Jews tried to cross the borders or escape by sea. Early in the war, Jews fleeing from Eastern Europe had passed through France to reach the United States by way of Spain. About 30,000 people escaped in this way. However, as the German noose tightened, the effort became more hazardous.

Harsh Occupation

After crushing the countries they invaded, the Germans set up occupation governments and instituted anti-Jewish laws. The occupation government in Holland was particularly harsh. Holland was declared a "protectorate" of Germany, and an Austrian named Arthur Seyss-Inquart was put in charge. He reported directly to Hitler and Himmler. His government deceived the Dutch, telling them that their cooperation would guarantee better treatment for citizens.

There, Jews were trapped inside a country without mountains or forested regions. Holland was also surrounded by German-controlled borders, and Germans patrolled the North Sea, cutting off that route to Great Britain. As a result, even though many non-Jews helped them, most Jews in Holland were doomed.

In November 1940, Jews and blacks in France were subjected to travel restrictions. After French police told German officials that there was no sure way to distinguish French Jews from others, Adolf Eichmann decided that Jews in all occupied countries must wear the yellow Star of David. The Vichy government, which had been fairly cooperative with the Germans, opposed the idea, as did Belgian authorities. Within two years, however, both countries would be forced to comply.

"A Time of Great Dread": Franz Werfel's Story

After France collapsed in June 1940, a Jewish writer named Franz Werfel and his wife tried to reach refuge in Portugal. Lacking visas or official paperwork, they were turned back. The Werfels found themselves once again in the French interior, among other Jewish refugees—Belgians, Dutch, French, Poles, Czechs, Austrians, and Germans. Werfel, however, was in special danger: His name was on a list of political enemies whom the Nazis planned to track down and execute.

Exhausted, and without food or shelter, the Werfels wandered the region around the Pyrenees Mountains. Then, a family in Pau told them to seek shelter in Lourdes, a nearby village that held a famous religious shrine that honored the Catholic saint Bernadette. For several weeks, the Werfels hid in the town. It was, Werfel later wrote, "a time of great dread." During those days, Werfel privately vowed that, if he ever reached the United States safely, he would write a book about Saint Bernadette and the miraculous events that were said to have occurred at Lourdes starting in the late 1800s.

By 1941, the Werfels were safe in California. Franz fulfilled his promise to write a book: *The Song of Bernadette* was highly praised and became a successful feature film. (Werfel actually smuggled part of the book over the Pyrenees, along with Gustav Mahler's Tenth Symphony.) In the preface, Werfel described his escape from Nazi persecution, saying,

I vowed that I would evermore and everywhere in all I wrote magnify the divine mystery and the holiness of man—careless of a period which has turned away with scorn and rage and indifference from these ultimate values. . . .

Vichy leaders debated what type of Jewish policy to enforce. Some wanted to pass laws against Jews and to deport those who were foreign-born. French Nazis wanted all Jews out of the country. At first, the government allowed foreign Jews to leave. In 1941, on its own, the Vichy government passed anti-Jewish laws. It would later help the Nazis round up Jews to be deported.

The Nazis spread a good deal of anti-Jewish propaganda in the occupied countries but were disappointed with the results. In 1941, Helmuth Knochen, commander of the SS for northern France and Belgium, complained, "It is almost impossible to cultivate in Frenchmen anti-Jewish feeling based on ideological grounds." The Nazis were also irritated when local police in occupied France did not help them to enforce anti-Jewish laws.

The Axis Is Formed

The autumn of 1940 saw Germany and Italy bolstering their alliance. On September 27, Italy, Germany, and Japan signed an agreement that formed the Rome-Berlin-Tokyo Axis. Italy had conquered parts of Africa (Libya, Somalia, and Ethiopia), so this agreement enlarged the war to that continent as well. Hungary, Romania, and Czechoslovakia—all of them linked to Germany— also signed this pact.

Now that Italy was an official ally of Germany, it saw a second wave of anti-Jewish persecution. Hitler pressured Mussolini to pass harsher laws against Jews. Among other things, the new laws deprived Jews of vending licenses and other types of work. "Many Jews fell into the most squalid misery," recalled Michele di Umberto, who lived with her family in the Rome ghetto. But fewer than one-quarter of all Italians supported the Fascist regime. Most Italians also opposed the persecution of Jews.

Mussolini ordered the Italian troops that had conquered Albania to invade Greece, where they met with utter defeat. In Egypt's desert, Italian forces were overwhelmed by British troops.

Now that he had achieved his major conquests in the west, Hitler turned his attention back to the east. Germany had formed a wobbly alliance with the Soviet Union, but secretly Hitler still detested the Soviets. He continued to talk of a "Jewish–Bolshevist conspiracy" that was supposedly based in the Soviet Union. Part of Hitler's renewed interest was the fact that he now needed larger supplies of food and fuel for his war effort. Control over the Soviet Union would provide Germany with vast agricultural areas and access to the rich oil fields of the Middle East. Against the advice of some of his generals, Hitler made plans to invade the Soviet Union. There, the Nazis would continue their push for world domination as they expanded persecution against the Jews, about 5 million of whom lived within Soviet borders.

"A Huge Game of Death"

Hitler and the Nazis had been in power for nearly eight years by 1941. Through unrelenting force, they had forced much of Europe to bend to their will. Clara Heller, who lived as a child in German-occupied Belgium, later observed:

[The Nazis'] tactics were aimed at creating confusion, indecision, insecurity, and general chaos in the Jewish community. It was as though we were taking part in a huge game of death. If a player could survive long enough, he might eventually figure out the rules. Unfortunately, few players remained after one or two rounds.

By 1941, nearly all Jews living in Nazi-dominated lands were trapped. The German government had stopped encouraging Jewish emigration. It now banned Jews from leaving. Jews were

----

Jews are marched through the streets of Cracow to a railway station, from which they will be deported to a death camp, 1941.

non-citizens; they could not even seek the protection of international laws.

Even so, people across Europe risked their lives to escape. Late in 1940, the *Salvador*—a ship carrying refugees—sank in the harbor off Istanbul, Turkey. The captain, who ran the vessel as a commercial business, asked the Turkish government to let him dock in Turkey during a storm, but he was turned down. The *Salvador* sank on December 12 in the Sea of Marmara; 231 refugees drowned.

Misery

Jews in the ghettos suffered new hardships early in 1941. During this time, the Nazis announced that ghetto residents must now give up all their coats and warm woolen garments to benefit German troops and civilians. People in the ghettos were already

----------- "We Are Striking on Behalf of the Jews" -------------

As 1941 began, the Nazi government in German-occupied Holland stepped up its persecution of Jews. In February, it demanded that all Jews register with the authorities. Leesha Rose wrote:

The decrees and orders against us were meant to destroy our pride and self-esteem. To refuse to carry out the Nazi decrees would be at the risk of being punished, imprisoned, or killed. . . . With keen psychological precision, they gradually stripped us of our rights, our social standing, and our worldly possessions.

A group of 425 Dutch Jews were arrested and sent to an Austrian camp called Mauthausen, where they were killed. Angry over the deaths and other Nazi actions, dockworkers in the Dutch capital, Amsterdam, called upon the Dutch people to hold a general strike, distributing flyers that said, "We are striking on behalf of the Jews, will you join?"

The strike lasted three days, but the Nazis subdued the defiance with brute force. People were shot in the streets, and more than 3,000 men were sent to concentration camps. Still, the strike had boosted morale, particularly among Jews.

By 1941, most ghettos were completely sealed off. This photo shows a footbridge used to get Jews from one side of the Lodz ghetto to the other. The street below is open to regular traffic.

suffering from the icy weather. Lacking coal and other fuel, most had to chop furniture and destroy buildings for their fires. They stuffed their clothing with paper and rags. People of all ages were freezing to death.

Disease and starvation in the ghettos continued to claim lives, as did unsanitary conditions. With no soap or hot water, people could not bathe, wash their hair, or clean their meager clothing. Toilets had been used beyond their limits and no longer worked; other plumbing equipment also broke down. Foul-smelling garbage piled up on the streets. The filth only increased the suffering of the Jews of the ghetto.

Typhus Rages

During the winter of 1940–1941, a typhus epidemic killed thousands. Typhus was the most prevalent of the many dangerous diseases that thrived in the ghetto. Those who caught typhus were separated from other people, and some were sent to the ghetto hospital. The hospital, however, had no medicine or equipment. Many patients grew even sicker there.

More than 100,000 people in the Warsaw ghetto would eventually contract typhus—and tens of thousands of them died. By June 1941, starvation had claimed another 20,000 lives.

Killing Squads Move In

On June 22, Germany began its long-planned invasion of the Soviet Union, called Operation Barbarossa. For this campaign, Hitler mobilized 3 million troops—nearly 80 percent of his entire army. Accompanying these troops were the dreaded *Einsatzgruppen*, the killing squads of the SS, who were now assigned to massacre Soviet Jews. The squads moved with terrifying precision through eastern Poland and the neighboring Soviet territories.

The Nazis no longer bothered to single out individuals or small groups for extermination; they massacred entire communities. After reaching a place where Jews lived, the Nazis told them they were being rounded up for "resettlement." One firing-squad commander later described how Jews were treated during these round-ups:

> *They were requested to hand over their valuables to the leaders of the unit and shortly before the execution to surrender their outer clothing. The men, women, and children were led to a place of execution which in most cases was located next to a more deeply excavated. . . . ditch. There they were shot, kneeling or standing, and the corpses thrown into a ditch.*

During these massacres, the victims were usually machine-gunned to death. They were killed either inside the huge pits or along the edges. Those who were wounded, but not killed outright, were buried alive. Some executions lasted for hours.

Other *Einsatzgruppen* killed victims inside special vans that functioned as moving gas chambers. People were locked inside and gas fumes piped in, causing death by a painful process of suffocation. As rumors spread about these vans, Jews began to hide when they spotted one on the road.

The cruelty and sadism of the execution tactics now reached even more severe levels. An eyewitness later described the barbarism he witnessed in a region of the Soviet Union. There, Jews were shot in trenches and sprayed with powdered lime, a caustic substance that burns flesh and causes bodies to decay. Row upon row of human beings were forced to lie on top of the dead so that they, too, could be shot. Children's heads were beaten against stones. Many were buried alive.

Red Friday

June 28, 1941, became known as "Red Friday." On that bleak day, Nazis burned the Jewish section in Bialystok, Poland, and forced more than 1,000 Jews inside a synagogue to burn with it. All of them were killed.

Some non-Jews witnessed the violence and heard the anguished cries of the victims. Yet only a few tried to help; they hid Jews or brought food to those who escaped into the woods. But most stood by and did nothing. Many feared that if they helped, they too would become victims.

This mass grave near Lvov, Poland, is filled with the victims of recent executions, 1941.

"Liquidate Ruthlessly"

Within just five weeks in mid-1941, the *Einsatzgruppen* killed more Jews than had died at the hands of the Nazis during all of the previous eight years. Other German troops helped them gather victims, and an additional 200,000 helpers came from local populations. In invaded Soviet territories,

Heinrich Himmler speaks with a young Soviet prisoner of war during a visit to a POW camp, 1941.

the *Einsatzgruppen* received more assistance from local collaborators than in any other land they had occupied. Also, the region provided many remote areas where people could be killed and buried.

In 1946, the Nuremberg International Tribunal, which investigated Nazi war crimes, found that the squads had received specific orders to carry out these massacres. The tribunal said that, in May 1941, Reinhard Heydrich, the deputy head of the SS, relayed the directives issued to him by Hitler himself. He told leaders of the killing squads to

> *...liquidate ruthlessly all opposition to National Socialism [Nazism]— not only the opposition of the present but that of the past and future as well. Whole categories of people were to be killed without truce, without investigation, without pity, tears or remorse. Women were to be slain with the men, and the children also were to be executed. . . .*

The tribunal estimated that approximately 2 million people were murdered by the *Einsatzgruppen*. The number murdered in the Soviet territories was estimated at more than 600,000.

People have struggled for decades to understand how ordinary people could carry out such crimes. The men who made up the *Einsatzgruppen* had previously been ordinary citizens, not criminals. Many were highly educated. Yet eyewitnesses and testimony from the men themselves show that they often brutalized and tortured people before killing them. In some cases, the killers even photographed their brutality; many proudly sent these photos home to Germany as souvenirs.

One of the most notorious squad leaders was Otto Ohlendorf. A former research economist, he had been put in charge of intelligence operations in 1939. After the war, Ohlendorf admitted that members of the *Einsatzgruppe* under his command had killed approximately 90,000 Jews.

Squad members later said that they were "only following orders" and tried not to think about what they were doing. Some said they drank in order to distance themselves from the reality of their mission. One squad member said, "During this time, we drank quite a lot. . . to stimulate our zeal for our work."

Nazis Move Toward Their "Final Solution"

The *Einsatzgruppen* were killing hundreds of thousands of Jews in a systematic program of mass murder. These rather primitive killing methods, however, were unsatisfactory to Hitler and other top-ranking Nazis. Among the problems they noted was the fact that some SS men refused to join the squads, while others did not want to continue. Military leaders said that it hurt the troops' morale to see women and children murdered.

The Germans estimated that about 11 million Jews now remained under their control. Millions of these Jews lived in big cities, where the killing squads could not operate in secret. Top Nazi officials now pondered more efficient, impersonal, and less costly methods of killing. The use of poison gas was discussed more and more frequently.

Auschwitz commandant Rudolf Höss would later say that, in the summer of 1941, Heinrich Himmler, the head of the SS, told him that Hitler had decided to use the labor camp at Auschwitz as the site for the mass destruction of European Jews. Hitler, he said, had given an order for a "final solution of the Jewish question." Höss was assigned to work out the details.

To test new methods of killing with gas, the Nazis constructed a special building at the camp in Chelmno. Several hundred Jews from small towns in that region were secretly killed there. That same summer, at Auschwitz–Birkenau (Birkenau, associated with the Auschwitz complex, was a camp built expressly for extermination), the Nazis tested pellets of cyanide gas called Zyklon B, a substance used to kill rats. The victims of this experiment were approximately 250 hospital patients and 600 Soviet prisoners of war.

The Nazis now began turning several concentration camps into outright death camps. To achieve their goal, they had only to identify—and transport—their millions of victims.

"Someday We Shall Pay for This"

In Poland, Jews were already labeled publicly for purposes of identification as well as humiliation. In September 1941, all Jews in German-occupied countries over six years of age were ordered to wear a yellow Star of David badge on their outer clothing at all times. The German word for "Jew"—*Jude*—was inscribed on the Star.

Eyewitnesses recorded the reactions of non-Jews after this decree took force. One Jew in Berlin thought that most people seemed embarrassed or even guilty. The majority tended to look away. Some Germans made a point of offering the Jews cigarettes or slipped candy or fruit into their pockets; others gave them seats on crowded trolleys. A German Army general wrote to relatives that requiring the wearing of the Star was "unworthy of an allegedly cultured nation. . . . Someday we shall pay for this."

Inge Auerbacher, who rode on a train each day to school, remembers being "taunted and heckled" by other children. Some people, however, showed compassion:

> One day a Christian woman left a bag of rolls next to my seat. She must have felt sorry for the little Jewish six-year-old traveling such a long distance by herself.

Outside Germany, reaction to this latest Nazi edict was mixed. Hubert Ripka, a member of the Czechoslovak National Committee, addressed Czechs over the BBC radio station out of London. He called the Star "a mark of honor which all decent people will respect." The Danish people, however, strongly disapproved. But in Eastern Europe, especially Poland, Jews found only a little support from editorials in the underground press.

Confined to the Ghetto

As fall arrived in 1941, Jews in Soviet territories were being thrust into newly formed ghettos. One of the largest was in Vilnius, the capital of Lithuania, once a great Jewish center of culture and learning. Tens of thousands of Jews were crowded into other ghettos in Lithuania, Latvia, and Russia. In Poland, Jews were told that they would be shot on sight if they strayed outside the walls of any ghetto.

Все жиды города Киева и его окрестностей должны явиться в понедельник 29 сентября 1941 года к 8 часам утра на угол Мельниковой и Доктеривской улиц (возле кладбищ).

Взять с собой документы, деньги и ценные вещи, а также теплую одежду, белье и пр.

Кто из жидов не выполнит этого распоряжения и будет найден в другом месте, будет расстрелян.

Кто из граждан проникнет в оставленные жидами квартиры и присвоит себе вещи, будет расстрелян.

This sign, posted in the Ukrainian city of Kiev in September 1941, orders Jews to assemble with their belongings. Anyone found not complying, it reads, "will be shot dead."

Despite the ghetto roundups, killing squads continued to find new victims. During the late summer, 500 people a day were being murdered at Ponary, a forest in Lithuania. Late in September, killing squads slaughtered 33,000 people at Babi Yar, near Kiev, in a period of two days. During September and October, the squads killed all the Jews of Estonia.

A letter dated October 27, 1941, reached leaders of the World Jewish Congress in Geneva, Switzerland. It described the horrifying ways in which people were being deported and dying in the

A Lithuanian collaborator stands guard over a group of prisoners from Vilnius, July 1941.

ghettos. Within a month, Jewish Agency representatives had sent a concerned message to Geneva, then on to Jerusalem. It said:

> With regard to the Jews, it seems that no place whatever has been allotted to them in Hitler's Europe, and the remnants who escaped the massacres, starvation, and oppression of the ghettos are no doubt intended to be sent somewhere overseas.

As yet, the World Jewish Congress and similar groups clearly had no idea about Hitler's "Final Solution." This process would take people to death camps instead of sending them overseas to start new lives.

Pearl Harbor

On December 7, 1941, Japanese bombers struck the U.S. naval base at Pearl Harbor, Hawaii. The next day, President Franklin D. Roosevelt made a speech summarizing the aggressions of Japan, Italy, and Germany. He concluded:

And what we have all learned is this: There is no such thing as security for any nation—or any individual—in a world ruled by the principles of gangsterism. . . . We are now in the midst of a war, not for conquest, not for vengeance, but for a world in which this nation, and all that this nation represents, will be safe for our children. We expect to eliminate the danger from Japan, but it would serve us ill if we accomplished that and found that the rest of the world was dominated by Hitler and Mussolini. We are going to win the war and we are going to win the peace that follows.

------------------------------ **"Save Us!"** ------------------------------

On December 12, 1941, a desperate group of 769 Romanian Jews boarded a run-down cattle boat named the S.S. *Struma*. It was bound for Palestine but broke down near Istanbul, Turkey. The ship and its passengers were forbidden to enter Turkey, and British authorities said that they could not come to Palestine.

International debate over the fate of the stranded refugees ensued, and the Zionist Emergency Committee in New York even offered to pay their expenses to Palestine. But the British government would not give in. For two months, the *Struma* stood in the water while helpless passengers held up a large sign that read SAVE US!

Meanwhile, conditions on the vessel were deteriorating rapidly. People were running out of food and, with every passing day, the ship became less seaworthy. Illnesses were also spreading.

The ship was still adrift in February 1942. At that point, it was pulled by tugboat out into the Black Sea, where it sank the next day. It was rumored that a Soviet submarine had sunk the boat. Only one passenger was known to have survived in the icy water.

In Germany, the family of Max Von Der Grun joined various people around the world who hoped that the war would soon end. His mother said, "The Americans will have chased Hitler to the devil."

On December 11, Hitler declared war on the United States. America, with its many airplanes, ships, factories, and raw materials, would be fighting both Japan and Germany. At the same time, Hitler faced fiercer opposition than he had expected on the Soviet front. Germans were being awakened many nights by the sound of Allied bombers and air-raid sirens. But their leaders assured them that all was well and that Germany was winning the war.

"Arm Yourselves Against Sympathy"

While the war escalated, the directors of the Auschwitz labor camp and members of the I.G. Farben company—which supervised the work camps—celebrated the holidays. The company's staff and Nazi officials held parties and ate a festive goose dinner.

Nearby, thousands of starving prisoners shivered in thin striped uniforms as they stood outside for daily roll calls. Those who did not stand upright or maintain the pace during work times knew they could be shot or gassed at the associated Birkenau death camp.

Regardless of what happened on the battlefield, the Nazis pursued the destruction of the Jews relentlessly. Their zeal was expressed by Hans Frank, the governor-general of the government set up by Germany in Poland. He told a group of SS leaders being assigned to various regions: "Gentlemen, I must ask you to arm yourselves against every feeling of sympathy. We must annihilate the Jews wherever we find them and wherever it is possible."

The years that would constitute the deadliest and most destructive era of the Holocaust had begun.

CHRONOLOGY OF THE HOLOCAUST: 1933–1945

1933

January 30
Adolf Hitler becomes chancellor of Germany

February 28
Nazis declare emergency after Reichstag fire; consolidate power

March 22
Nazis open first concentration camp: Dachau

May 10
Public book burnings target works by Jews and opponents of the Nazis

July 14
Nazi Party established as one and only legal party in Germany
···▶

1934

January 26
German–Polish non-aggression pact signed
···▶

1935

September 15
Nuremberg Laws passed
···▶

1936

March
Germany occupies Rhineland, flouting the Versailles Treaty
⋮
↓

August
Olympic Games held in Berlin
◀····

1938

November 9–10
Kristallnacht: long-planned pogrom explodes across "Greater Germany"

September 29
Munich Conference: appeasement; Allies grant Germany Sudetenland (part of Czechoslovakia)

July 6–13
Evian Conference: refugee policies

March 13
Anschluss: annexation of Austria

1937

September 7
Hitler declares end of the Versailles Treaty
◀····

⋮
↓

1939

May
British White Paper: Jewish emigration to Palestine limited
···▶

August 23
Soviet–German non-aggression pact signed

September 1
Germany invades Poland; Poland falls within a month

September 2
Great Britain and France declare war on Germany

September 17
Red (Soviet) Army invades eastern Poland

October 8
First ghetto established in Poland
⋮
↓

1941

June 22
Operation Barbarossa: invasion of the Soviet Union; German war on two fronts

March 24
Germany invades North Africa

1940

October 16
Order for creation of Warsaw ghetto
◀···

April 27
Heinrich Himmler orders creation of Auschwitz concentration camp; established May 20

Spring
Germany conquers Denmark, Norway, Belgium, Luxembourg, Holland, and France (occupies northern part)

February 12
Deportation of Jews from Germany to occupied Poland begins

⋮

July 31
Reinhard Heydrich appointed to implement "Final Solution": extermination of European Jewry

December 7
Japan attacks Pearl Harbor

December 11
Germany and Italy declare war on the United States
···▶

1942

January 20
Wannsee Conference: coordination of "Final Solution"

Spring–Summer
Liquidation of Polish ghettos; deportation of Jews to extermination camps

November 19–20
Soviet Army counterattacks at Stalingrad
⋮
↓

1944

May–July
Deportation of Hungarian Jews: 437,402 sent to Auschwitz

June 6
D-Day: Allies invade Normandy

July
Soviet troops liberate Majdanek camp in Poland

October 2
Danes rescue more than 7,200 Jews from Nazis
◀···

June 11
Heinrich Himmler orders liquidation of all ghettos in Poland and the Soviet Union

April 19–May 16
Warsaw ghetto uprising

April 19
Bermuda Conference: fruitless discussion of rescue of Jewish victims of Nazis; liquidation of Warsaw ghetto begins

1943

January 18–21
Major act of resistance in Warsaw ghetto
◀····

1945

January 27
Soviet troops liberate Auschwitz–Birkenau
···▶

April–May
Allies liberate Buchenwald, Bergen-Belsen, Dachau, Mauthausen, and Theresienstadt concentration camps

April 30
Hitler commits suicide

May 7
Germany surrenders unconditionally to Allies

May 8
V-E Day: Victory in Europe
⋮
↓

November
Nuremberg Trials begin

Glossary

Anschluss The German invasion and annexation of Austria on March 12–13, 1938.

Anti-Semite A person who hates Jews.

Antisemitism Hatred of Jews.

Aryanization A term used by the Nazis to mean the transfer of all assets and control of German-owned businesses to Germans who were considered Aryans.

Aryans Originally, a term referring to speakers of any Indo-European language. The Nazis used the term to mean people of Northern European background, or members of what the Nazis termed the German "master race."

Communism A political, social, and economic ideology that aims for a classless society. German Communists were the first opponents of the Nazis.

Concentration Camps Labor camps set up by the Nazis to house political prisoners or people they considered to be "undesirable." Prisoners were made to work like slaves and many died as a result of starvation, disease, or beatings. *Also called work camps, work centers, and prison camps.*

Einsatzgruppen "Special Action Groups" or killing squads. Part of the SS, their main purpose was to kill enemies of the Reich, especially Jews and Communists.

Extermination Camps Death camps built by the Nazis in German-occupied Poland for the sole purpose of killing "enemies" of the Third Reich. The victims' bodies were usually burned in ovens (crematoria). The six extermination camps were Auschwitz–Birkenau, Belzec, Chelmno, Majdanek, Sobibór, and Treblinka. *Also called killing centers.*

Fascism A political philosophy or system that values a nation, and often a particular group, above the individual; and which has an autocratic, centralized government, usually headed by a dictator.

Führer A German word meaning "leader." It was used to refer to Adolf Hitler, dictator of Germany from 1933 to 1945, and head of the Nazi Party.

Gentile A non-Jewish person.

Gestapo The Nazi secret police who were responsible for rounding up, arresting, and deporting victims to ghettos or camps. The Gestapo were part of the SS.

Ghetto In Hitler's Europe, the section of a city where Jews were forced to live apart from other groups, in conditions of extreme crowding and deprivation.

Holocaust A term for the state-sponsored, systematic persecution and annihilation of European Jewry by Nazi Germany and its collaborators between 1933 and 1945. While Jews were the primary victims, with approximately 6 million murdered, many other groups were targeted, including Romani, the mentally and physically disabled, Soviet prisoners of war, political dissidents, Jehovah's Witnesses, and male homosexuals. It is estimated that perhaps as many as 4 million non-Jews were killed under the Nazi regime.

Jews People who belong to the religion of Judaism.

Kristallnacht "Night of Broken Glass," or "Night of Crystal," more correctly termed the "November Pogroms." November 9-10, 1938, a night of Nazi-planned terror throughout Germany and Austria, when Jews were attacked and arrested and their property destroyed.

Lebensraum A German term for "living space" to accommodate what the Nazis called the "master race" of Aryan people.

Munich Pact A treaty by which Great Britain and France agreed not to resist Germany's occupation of Sudetenland in 1938. *Also called Munich Agreement.*

Nazi A term describing a member of the Nazi Party or something associated with the party, such as "Nazi government."

Nazi Party Short for the National Socialist German Workers' Party. Founded in 1919, the party became a potent political force under Hitler's leadership.

Nuremberg Laws "Reich Citizenship Laws," passed on September 15, 1935. These sweeping laws specified the qualifications for German citizenship and excluded from citizenship persons of Jewish ancestry.

Palestine A region in the Middle East, part of which is now known as Israel. Palestine was controlled by the British government from 1922 to 1948.

Pogroms Organized, mass attacks against a group of people. Carried out by the Nazis against those they considered inferior, particularly Jews.

Propaganda The deliberate spreading of ideas, information or rumors—often false—for the purpose of helping or injuring a cause, organization, or person.

Reichstag The German Parliament.

Resistance A general term for actions taken by individuals in various countries, both Jews and Gentiles, against the Nazis. Members of resistance groups worked "underground," in secrecy.

Rhineland A region between Germany and France that was demilitarized after World War I as a buffer zone to prevent another German invasion.

Swastika An ancient design that the Nazis adapted for their party symbol.

SS From the German term *Schutzstaffel,* meaning "defense unit." The SS began as Hitler's personal bodyguard and developed into the most powerful and feared organization in the Third Reich. *Also called black-shirts.*

Star of David The six-pointed star that is a symbol of Judaism.

Sudetenland The western part of Czechoslovakia along the border of Germany that was invaded and occupied by Germany in 1938.

Third Reich *Reich* means "empire." In German history, the First Reich lasted from 962 until 1806, the second from 1871 to 1918. In the early 1920s, Hitler began using the term "Third Reich" to describe his own empire, which lasted from 1933 until 1945.

Treaty of Versailles The 1919 peace treaty that ended World War I. In it, the conditions of surrender for Germany and the Axis powers were outlined.

Untermenschen A German word meaning "subhumans," used by the Nazis to refer to some groups they considered "undesirable"—Jews, Romani, male homosexuals, political opponents, and the physically and mentally disabled.

Source Notes

Introduction:

p. 9: "We wish you…." Ina R. Friedman. *Escape or Die.* Reading, MA: Addison-Wesley, 1982, p. 17.

p. 10: "Destroy everything…." Ina R. Friedman, p. 17.

p. 12: "Hang them!" David Adler. *We Remember the Holocaust.* New York: Henry Holt, 1989, p. 18.

p. 13: "Utter madness…." Scholasticus. "When Hitler Got a Hero's Welcome." *New England Monthly,* April 1990, p. 24.

p. 15: "…fire and the sword." John V.H. Dippel. *Bound Upon a Wheel of Fire.* New York: Basic Books, 1996, p. 249.

p. 15: "an insane whirlwind…." Vera Laska. *Women of the Resistance.* Westport, CT: Greenwood Press, 1983, p. xiv.

p. 15: "It is beside the point…." Milton Meltzer. *Never to Forget: The Jews of the Holocaust.* New York: Harper & Row, 1976, p. 20.

Chapter 1:

p. 18: "peace in our time…." Burton H. Wolfe. *Hitler and the Nazis.* G.P. Putnam's Sons, 1970, p. 154.

p. 20: "Antisemitism is not…." Philip Friedman. *Their Brothers' Keepers.* New York: Holocaust Library, 1978, p. 101.

p. 20: "Germans had torn…." Ina R. Friedman, p. 44.

p. 21: "calm, order, and peace…." and "take the Czech people…." William Shirer. *The Nightmare Years.* New York: Simon & Schuster, 1984, p. 380.

p. 21: "For the Czechs a long night…." Shirer, p. 381.

p. 23: "His Majesty's government…." Ruth Kluger and Peggy Mann. *The Secret Ship.* New York: Doubleday, 1978, p. 118.

p. 25: "In May 1939…." Inge Auerbacher. *I Am a Star: Child of the Holocaust.* New York: Prentice-Hall, 1985, p. 23.

p. 26: "I would never…." Auerbacher, p. 28.

p. 27: "Alex, what you are after…." James M. Burns. *Roosevelt: The Soldier of Freedom.* New York: Harcourt, Brace, 1973, p. 250.

Chapter 2:

p. 30: Close your eyes…." Robert Goldston. *The Life and Death of Nazi Germany.* New York: Fawcett, 1967, p. 128.

p. 30: "It is evil things…." Lucy S. Dawidowicz. *The War Against the Jews, 1933–1945.* New York: Holt, Rinehart, & Winston, 1975, p. 111.

p. 31: "It was a close…." David Adler, p. 54.

p. 33: "We shall have…." Ina R. Friedman, p. 31.

p. 34: "Poles are...." Thomas E. Wood. *Karski: How One Man Tried to Stop the Holocaust.* New York: Wiley and Sons, 1994, p. 34.

p. 35: "the doctrine that it is...." Gail B. Stewart. *Life in the Warsaw Ghetto.* San Diego: Lucent Books, 1992, p. 37.

p. 36: "We could not walk...." Rhoda G. Lewin, ed. *Witnesses to the Holocaust.* Boston: Twayne Publishers, 1991, p. 20.

p. 36: "...make men of us...." Wood, p. 34.

p. 37: "Of all the native police...." Raul Hilberg. *Victims, Perpetrators, Bystanders.* New York: HarperCollins, 1992, p. 92.

p. 39: "final aim...." and "to be kept...." Benjamin B. Ferencz. *Less Than Slaves.* Cambridge, MA: Harvard University Press, 1979, p. 13.

Chapter 3:

p. 41: Description of those the Nazis deemed unfit for life in Laska, p. 14.

p. 41: "When a German...." Raul Hilberg. *The Destruction of the European Jews.* New York: Holmes & Meier, 1985, p. 489.

p. 42: "the national economy." Dawidowicz, p. 114.

p. 42: "the housecleaning of...." Meltzer, p. 65.

p. 44: "in an endless stream...." Martin Gilbert. *The Holocaust.* New York: Holt, Rinehart, & Winston, 1985, pp. 129–130.

p. 46: "Every day when you walked...." Adler, p. 60.

p. 47: "I made use of...." Barbara Rogasky. *Smoke and Ashes: The Story of the Holocaust.* New York: Holiday House, 1988, p. 45.

p. 47: "In 1940, as they...." and "In 1940 the Germans...." Samuel Oliner and Pearl Oliner. *The Altruistic Personality: Rescuers of Jews in Nazi Europe.* New York: The Free Press, 1992, p. 119.

p. 49: "They love life...." Stewart, p. 73.

p. 49: "The devil himself...." Meltzer, p. 80.

Chapter 4:

p. 51: "The sides...." Leni Yahil. *The Holocaust: The Fate of European Jewry.* New York: Oxford University Press, 1990, p. 240.

p. 54: "They would not...." Klüger, pp. 78–79.

p. 54: "To keep going...." Klüger, p. 103.

p. 55: "The German planes...." Leesha Rose. *The Tulips Are Red.* New York: A.S. Barnes and Co., 1978, pp. 18–19.

pp. 55–56: "Even though large...." Wolfe, p. 175.

p. 58: "A time of great dread...." Franz Werfel. *The Song of Bernadette.* New York: Viking, 1942, p. 6.

p. 58: "I vowed...." Werfel, p. 7.

pp. 58–59: "It is almost impossible...." Philip Friedman, p. 45.

p. 59: "Many Jews fell into...." Alexander Stille. *Benevolence and Betrayal: Five Italian Jewish Families Under Fascism.* New York: Simon & Schuster, 1991, p. 181.

Chapter 5:

p. 61: "[The Nazis'] tactics...." Clara Isaacman. *Clara's Story.* Philadelphia: The Jewish Publication Society, 1984, p. 81.

p. 62: "The decrees...." Rose, p. 29.

p. 63: Statistics on typhus, starvation, Adler, p. 62.

p. 64: "they were requested...." Dawidowicz, p. 167.

p. 66: "...liquidate ruthlessly...." Ferencz, p. 11.

p. 67: "During this time...." Rogasky, p. 51.

p. 67: "final solution of...." Rudolf Höss. *Kommandant in Auschwitz.* Stuttgart: Deutsche Verlag, 1958, pp. 175–176.

p. 68: Reactions of non-Jews in Philip Friedman, p. 34.

p. 68: "One day...." Auerbacher, p. 28.

p. 68: "a mark of honor...." Philip Friedman, p. 36.

p. 70: "With regard to the Jews...." Central Zionist Archives, Z 4/14779, cited in Martin Gilbert. *Auschwitz and the Allies.* New York: Holt, Rinehart, & Winston, 1981, p. 17.

p. 71: "And what we have all learned...." The correspondents of *Time, Life,* and *Fortune. December 7, The First Thirty Hours.* New York: Alfred A. Knopf, 1942, pp. 190–192.

p. 72: "The Americans...." Max Von Der Grun. *Howl Like the Wolves: Growing Up in Nazi Germany.* Trans. Jan Van Heurk. New York: William Morrow, 1980, p. 208.

p. 75: Statistics from Gilbert, *Auschwitz and the Allies,* p. 15.

Bibliography

David A. Adler. *We Remember the Holocaust.* New York: Henry Holt, 1989.

Stanislaw Adler. *In the Warsaw Ghetto, 1940-1943.* Jerusalem: Yad Vashem, 1982.

Inge Auerbacher. *I Am a Star: Child of the Holocaust.* New York: Prentice-Hall, 1985.

Yehuda Bauer. *A History of the Holocaust.* New York: Franklin Watts, 1982.

Norman H. Baynes, ed. *The Speeches of Adolf Hitler.* New York: Howard Fertig, 1969.

Mary Berg. *Warsaw Ghetto Diary.* New York: L. B. Fischer, 1945.

Alan Bullock. *Hitler: A Study in Tyranny.* New York: Harper and Row, 1971.

Alan Bullock. *Hitler and Stalin: Parallel Lives.* New York: Alfred A. Knopf, Inc., 1992.

James M. Burns. *Roosevelt: The Soldier of Freedom.* New York: Harcourt, Brace, 1973.

Miriam Chaikin. *A Nightmare in History: The Holocaust 1933–1945.* New York: Clarion, 1987.

Stacy Cretzmeyer. *Your Name is Renee: Ruth's Story as a Hidden Child.* Brunswick, ME: Biddle Publishing, 1994.

Lucy S. Dawidowicz. *The War Against the Jews 1933–1945.* New York: Holt, Rinehart, & Winston, 1975.

John V.H. Dippel. *Bound Upon a Wheel of Fire.* New York: Basic Books, 1996.

Benjamin B. Ferencz. *Less Than Slaves.* Cambridge, MA: Harvard University Press, 1979.

Edward H. Flannery. *The Anguish of the Jews.* New York: Paulist Press, 1985.

Eva Fogelman. *Conscience and Courage.* New York: Doubleday, 1994.

Ina R. Friedman. *Escape or Die: True Stories of People Who Survived the Holocaust.* Reading, MA: Addison-Wesley, 1982.

Philip Friedman. *Roads to Extinction: Essays on the Holocaust.* New York: The Jewish Publication Society, 1980.

Philip Friedman. *Their Brothers' Keepers.* new York: Holocaust Library, 1978.

Miep Gies and Alison L. Gold. *Anne Frank Remembered.* New York: Simon & Schuster, 1988.

Martin Gilbert. *Auschwitz and the Allies.* New York: Holt, Rinehart, & Winston, 1981.

Martin Gilbert. *The Holocaust.* New York: Holt, Rinehart, & Winston, 1985.

Robert Goldston. *The Life and Death of Nazi Germany.* New York: Fawcett, 1967.

Sarah Gordon. *Hitler, Germans, and the "Jewish Question."* Princeton, NJ: Princeton University Press, 1984.

Yisrael Gutman. *The Jews of Warsaw: 1939–1943.* Bloomington, IN: Indiana University Press, 1982.

Raul Hilberg. *The Destruction of the European Jews.* New York: Holmes & Meier, 1985.

Raul Hilberg. *Victims, Perpetrators, and Bystanders.* New York: HarperCollins, 1992.

Adolf Hitler. *Mein Kampf.* Trans. by Ralph Manheim. Boston: Houghton Mifflin, 1943.

Clara Isaacman. *Clara's Story.* Philadelphia: The Jewish Publication Society, 1984.

Chaim Kaplan. *Scroll of Agony: The Warsaw Diary of Chaim Kaplan.* New York: Collier, 1965.

Ruth Kluger and Peggy Mann. *The Secret Ship.* New York: Doubleday, 1978.

Elaine Landau. *We Survived the Holocaust.* New York: Franklin Watts, 1991.

Vera Laska. *Women of the Resistance.* Westport, CT: Greenwood Press, 1983.

Nora Levin. *The Holocaust: The Destruction of European Jewry, 1933-1945.* New York: Crowell, 1968.

Abraham Lewin. *A Cup of Tears: A Diary of the Warsaw Ghetto.* Oxford, England: Basil Blackwell, 1988.

Rhoda G. Lewin, ed. *Witnesses to the Holocaust.* Boston: Twayne Publishers, 1991.

Milton Meltzer. *Never to Forget: The Jews of the Holocaust.* New York: Harper & Row, 1976.

Samuel Oliner and Pearl Oliner. *The Altruistic Personality: Rescuers of Jews in Nazi Europe.* New York: The Free Press, 1992.

Abraham Resnick. *The Holocaust.* San Diego, CA: Lucent Books, 1991.

Hans Peter Richter. *I Was There.* New York: Holt, Rinehart, Winston, 1972.

Carol Rittner and John K. Roth, eds. *Different Voices: Women and the Holocaust.* New York: Paragon House, 1993.

Barbara Rogasky. *Smoke and Ashes: The Story of the Holocaust.* New York: Holiday House, 1988.

Charles G. Roland. *Courage Under Siege: Starvation, Disease, and Death in the Warsaw Ghetto.* New York: Oxford University Press, 1992.

Leesha Rose. *The Tulips are Red.* New York: A.S. Barnes and Co., 1978, pp. 18–19.

Seymour Rossel. *The Holocaust.* New York: Franklin Watts, 1981.

Margaret L. Rossiter. *Women in the Resistance.* New York: Praeger, 1986.

Arnold Rubin. *The Evil Men Do: The Story of the Nazis.* New York: Julian Messner, 1977.

William Shirer. *The Nightmare Years.* New York: Simon & Schuster, 1984.

William Shirer. *The Rise and Fall of the Third Reich.* New York: Simon & Schuster, 1959.

Bea Stadtler. *The Holocaust: A History of Courage and Resistance.* New York: Behrman House, 1973.

Gail B. Stewart. *Life in the Warsaw Ghetto.* San Diego, CA: Lucent Books, 1992.

Alexander Stille. *Benevolence and Betrayal: Five Italian Jewish Families Under Fascism.* New York: Simon & Schuster, 1991.

Max Von Der Grun. *Howl Like the Wolves: Growing Up in Nazi Germany.* Trans. by Jan Van Heurk. New York: William Morrow, 1980.

Franz Werfel. *The Song of Bernadette.* New York: Viking, 1942.

Burton H. Wolfe. *Hitler and the Nazis.* G.P. Putnam's Sons, 1970.

Thomas E. Wood. *Karski: How One Man Tried to Stop the Holocaust.* New York: Wiley and Sons, 1994.

Leni Yahil. *The Holocaust: The Fate of European Jewry.* New York: Oxford University Press, 1990.

Susan Zuccotti. *The Italians and the Holocaust.* New York: Basic Books, 1987.

Articles:

Omer Bartov. "Ordinary Monsters." *The New Republic*, April 29, 1996, pp. 32–38.

"Blitzkrieg." *Time.* August 28, 1989.

Peter Plagens. "A Birthday Trip in Hell." *Newsweek*, September 10, 1990, pp. 54–55.

Scholasticus. "When Hitler Got a Hero's Welcome." *New England Monthly*, April 1990, pp. 24–25.

Fritz Stern. "The Goldhagen Controversy." *The New Republic*, November/December 1996, pp. 128–138.

Further Reading

David A. Adler. *We Remember the Holocaust.* New York: Henry Holt, 1989.

Inge Auerbacher. *I Am a Star: Child of the Holocaust.* New York: Prentice-Hall, 1985.

Miriam Chaikin. *A Nightmare in History: The Holocaust 1933–1945.* New York: Clarion, 1987.

Stacy Cretzmeyer. *Your Name is Renee: Ruth's Story as a Hidden Child.* Brunswick, ME: Biddle Publishing, 1994.

Ina R. Friedman. *Escape or Die: True Stories of People Who Survived the Holocaust.* Reading, MA: Addison-Wesley, 1982.

Miep Gies and Alison L. Gold. *Anne Frank Remembered.* New York: Simon & Schuster, 1988.

Raul Hilberg. *Victims, Perpetrators, and Bystanders.* New York: HarperCollins, 1992.

Clara Isaacman. *Clara's Story.* Philadelphia: The Jewish Publication Society, 1984.

Ruth Kluger and Peggy Mann. *The Secret Ship.* New York: Doubleday, 1978.

Elaine Landau. *We Survived the Holocaust.* New York: Franklin Watts, 1991.

Milton Meltzer. *Never to Forget: The Jews of the Holocaust.* New York: Harper & Row, 1976.

Joachim Remak. *The Nazi Years: A Documentary History.* New York: Harper & Row, 1976.

Hans Peter Richter. *I Was There.* New York: Holt, Rinehart, Winston, 1972.

Barbara Rogasky. *Smoke and Ashes: The Story of the Holocaust.* New York: Holiday House, 1988.

Seymour Rossel. *The Holocaust.* New York: Franklin Watts, 1981.

Arnold Rubin. *The Evil Men Do: The Story of the Nazis.* New York: Julian Messner, 1977.

Bea Stadtler. *The Holocaust: A History of Courage and Resistance.* New York: Behrman House, 1973.

Gail B. Stewart. *Life in the Warsaw Ghetto.* San Diego, CA: Lucent Books, 1992.

Max Von Der Grun. *Howl Like the Wolves: Growing Up in Nazi Germany.* Trans. by Jan Van Heurk. New York: William Morrow, 1980.

Index

A

Ali, Rashid, 26
Altusky, Hirsh, 46
Anschluss, 13
Antisemitism
description and history of,
11–12
Atomic bomb, 27
Auerbacher, Inge, 24–26, 68
Auschwitz–Birkenau concentra-
tion camp, 32, 68
Austria, Nazi violence in, 13
Axis powers, formation of, 59

B

Balfour Declaration of 1917, 23
Beck, Ludwig, 18
Belgium, German invasion of, 53
Benes, Eduard, 19
Benites, Manuel, 24
Black-shirts, 41–42, 64–67
Brown-shirts, 11

C

Chamberlain, Neville, 18, 20, 30
China, Jewish asylum in, 22
Chronology of Holocaust, 73
Churchill, Winston, 23, 55–56
Concentration camps
Auschwitz–Birkenau, 32, 68
establishment of, 12–13
Cracow ghetto, **47**
See also Ghettos, Jewish
Cremation, 43
"Crystal Night." *See Kristallnacht*
Cuban reaction to Jewish
refugees, 24–25
Czechoslovakia, German
invasion of, 19–21, 26

D

"Death boxes." *See* Ghettos,
Jewish
Deportations
of Czechoslovakian Jews, 26
of Polish Jews, 34
Di Umberto, Michele, 59

E

Eichmann, Adolf, 21, 39
Eiger, David, 36

Einsatzgruppen, 41–42, 64–67
Einstein, Albert, **27**
Epidemic, typhus, 63–64
Evian Conference, 22
Experiments, medical, 48

F

Foreign reaction to
Hitler's aggression, 20
Jewish refugees, 18, 22–26
Nazism, 18
France, German invasion of,
56–57
Frank, Anne, Edith, Margot,
and Otto, 55
Frank, Hans, 72

G

Gale, Manny, 9–10, 19
Gassing of Jews, 43, 67–68
Gentiles reluctance to help Jews,
37
Germany
Hitler's Reich, 14 (map)
invasion of neighboring
countries, 15, 18–21, 26–27,
29–32, 52–53, 55–59, 64
Gestapo, role of, 39
Ghettos, Jewish
conditions in, 43–47, 49,
62–63, 69–70
Goebbels, Josef, 12
Gotthold, Helene, 33
Graves, mass, 64, **65**
Great Britain
German invasion of, 56
reaction to Jewish refugees,
23–24
Grun, Max Von Der, 72
Grynszpan, Herschel, 13
Gypsies. *See* Romani

H

Haakon VII, King of Norway, 52
Hacha, Emil, 19–21
Hamada, Carl, 31
Heller, Clara, 61
Heydrich, Reinhard, 39, 42, 66
Hilberg, Raul, 37
Himmler, Heinrich, 34, 39, **66**, 67
Hindenburg, Paul von, 11
Hitler, Adolf, **8**, **13**, **56**
master plan, 15

rise to power, 10–11
view of Jews, 11
war on United States, 72
See also Nazi Party; Nazis
Holland, German invasion of,
53, 55, 57
Holocaust, chronology of, 73
Höss, Rudolf, 67

I

I Am a Star (Auerbacher), 24–26,
68

J

Jehovah's Witnesses, persecution
of, 33
Jews
exodus from Germany, 17–18
gassing of, 43, 67–68
increasing violence against,
13–14, 21, 35–36
Judenrat, 21, 45

K

Kaplan, Chaim, 49, 51
Karski, Jan, 34
Killing squads, 41–42, 64–67
Kluger, Ruth, 54
Knochen, Helmuth, 58
Kristallnacht, 9–10, 14

L

Laredo Bru, Federico, 24
Laws, anti-Jewish, 12–13, 36, 48
Liebschutz Rosza, Lisa, 20, 26
"Lightening War" with Poland,
30
Lodz ghetto, 43–44, **45**, **46**, **63**
See also Ghettos, Jewish
Luxembourg, German invasion
of, 53

M

Manhattan Project, 27
"Master Race," 42
Medical experiments performed
on Jews, 48
Mentally disabled people, mur-
dering of, 42–43
Metzen, Frieda, 33
Molotov, Vyacheslav, **16**
Mussolini, Benito, 17, 30, 59

N

National Socialist German
  Workers' Party. *See* Nazi Party
Nazi Party
  origination of, 11
  See also Hitler, Adolf
Nazis
  gassing of Jews, 43
  invasion of neighboring
    countries, 15, 18–21, 26–27,
    29–32, 52–53, 55–59, 64
  organized attacks on Jews, 13
  See also Hitler, Adolf
"Night of Broken Glass." *See*
  Kristallnacht
Non-Jews
  persecution of, 33, 48
  reluctance to help Jews, 37
November Pogroms, 9–10, 14
Nuremberg International
  Tribunal, 66
Nuremberg Laws, 12–13, 48

P

Palestine immigration of Jews, 23
Pearl Harbor, 71
Petain, Marshal, 57
Pogrom, 13
Poland
  German invasion of, 27, 29–32
  Jewish culture, 31
Nazification of, 34–37

R

Red Friday, 65

Refugees, Jewish, 18, 22–26, 54,
  62
Religion, Nazi opposition to, 33
Resistance groups, 62
Ribbentrop, Joachim von, **16**
Ripka, Hubert, 68
Romani, **48**
Roosevelt, Franklin D., 22–23,
  25, 27, 71
Rose, Leesha, 53, 62

S

Sachs, Alexander, 27
Salvador (ship), sinking of, 62
SA (*Sturmabteilungen*), 11
Scandinavian countries, German
  invasion of, 52–53
Seyss-Inquart, Arthur, 57
Shanghai, Jewish asylum in, 22
Shirer, William, 21
Sosnowski, Piotr, **33**
Soviet Union
  German invasion of, 59
  non-aggression pact with
    Hitler, 26–27, 31
"Special Duty" Squads, 41–42,
  64–67
SS (*Schutzstaffel*), 41–42, 64–67
St. Louis (ship), 24–**25**
Stalin, Joseph, **16**
Star of David, 21, 37, 68
Sterilization, 42
Struma (ship), sinking of, 71
Sudetenland, Hitler's annexation
  of, 18

Szilard, Leo, 27

T

T-4 Program, 42–43
Treaty of Versailles, 10–11, 18
Typhus epidemic, 63–64

U

United States
  Hitler's declaration of war on,
    72
  reaction to Jewish refugees,
    23
Untermenschen, 41

V

Vans, gassing, 64
Versailles, Treaty of, 10–11, 18

W

Warsaw ghetto, **40**, 44–47, **49**
  See also Ghettos, Jewish
Werfel, Franz, 58
"White Paper," 23
Wilhelmina, Queen of Holland,
  53
World War I, 10–11
World War II, 30

Y

Yellow star, 68–69

Z

Zyklon B, 68

Photo Credits

Cover: AP/Wide World Photos; pages 8, 9: Richard Freimark, courtesy of USHMM Photo Archives; page 13: Dokumentationsarchiv des Österreichischen Widerstandes, courtesy of USHMM Photo Archives; pages 16, 17, 25, 50, 51, 56, 66: National Archives, courtesy of USHMM Photo Archives; pages 27, 29, 30, 40, 41: Courtesy of USHMM Photo Archives; page 32: Yad Vashem Photo Archives, courtesy of USHMM Photo Archives; pages 33, 35 (middle), 38, 65: Main Commission for the investigation of Nazi War Crimes, courtesy of USHMM Photo Archives; page 35 (top): Bildarchiv Preussischer Kulturbesitz, courtesy of USHMM Photo Archives; page 35 (bottom): Jewish Historical Institute Warsaw, courtesy of USHMM Photo Archives; page 44: National Archives in Krakow, courtesy of USHMM Photo Archives; page 45: Raphael Aronson, courtesy of USHMM Photo Archives; page 46: YIVO Institute for Jewish Research, courtesy of USHMM Photo Archives; pages 47, 60, 61: State Archive—Krakow, courtesy of USHMM Photo Archives; page 48: Archives of Mechanical Documentation, courtesy of USHMM Photo Archives; page 49: Gunther Schwarberg, courtesy of USHMM Photo Archives; page 52: Francisca Verdonner Kan, courtesy USHMM Photo Archives; page 63: Main Crimes Commission, courtesy of USHMM Photo Archives; page 69: Jewish Cultural Society of Kiev, courtesy of USHMM Photo Archives; page 70: Bundersarchiv, courtesy of USHMM Photo Archives.

All maps and graphs ©Blackbirch Press, Inc.